HOME WORKSHOP GUNS

Volume V

The AR-15/M16

GUNS
for Defense and Resistance

HOME WORKSHOP GUNS

Volume V

The AR-15/M16

GUNS

for Defense and Resistance

Bill Holmes

PALADIN PRESS • BOULDER, COLORADO

The Home Workshop Guns for Defense and Resistance series:

Vol. I: The Submachine Gun
Vol. II: The Handgun
Vol. III: The .22 Machine Pistol
Vol. IV: The 9mm Machine Pistol
Home Workshop Prototype Firearms
Home Workshop Weaponry (video)
Home Workshop .50-Caliber Sniper Rifle (video)
.50-Caliber Rifle Construction Manual
A Master's Guide to Building Bolt-Action Rifles

Home Workshop Guns for Defense and Resistance, Vol. V: The AR-15/M16
by Bill Holmes

Copyright © 1997 by Bill Holmes
ISBN 13: 978-0-87364-948-3
Printed in the United States of America

Published by Paladin Press, a division of
Paladin Enterprises, Inc.,
Gunbarrel Tech Center
7077 Winchester Circle
Boulder, Colorado 80301 USA
+1.303.443.7250

Direct inquiries and/or orders to the above address.

Visit our Web site at www.paladin-press.com

TABLE OF CONTENTS

WARNING

Although at the time this book was written it was perfectly legal for an individual to manufacture a firearm for personal use, experimental purposes, or research and development, it is likely that new laws have been added since. It is probably still legal for the upper receiver assemblies described in this book to be built and assembled on an existing lower receiver. However, if the lower receiver, as described herein, is used, an illegal firearm will result. It is the reader's obligation to carefully research all pertinent laws before any such construction is attempted.

Technical data presented here, particularly data on ammunition and on the construction, use, adjustment, and alteration of firearms, inevitably reflects the author's individual beliefs and experiences with particular firearms, equipment, and components under specific circumstances that the reader cannot duplicate exactly. The information in this book should therefore be used for guidance only and approached with great caution. Neither the author, publisher, nor distributors assume any responsibility for the use or misuse of information contained in this book. *This book is presented for academic study only.*

PREFACE

If my memory serves me correctly, it was in early 1980 that someone suggested to me that a 9mm conversion unit to mate with and mount on an AR-15 or M16 lower receiver assembly would be desirable. A bit of research on my part indicated that there was indeed a market for such a conversion.

At the time I thought it best to use square tubing for the upper receiver since it was possible to get more weight into a square bolt of the maximum permissible length than a round one. A bushing was welded into the front end of the receiver tube and bored and threaded to accept a removable barrel. This was held in place by a barrel-retaining nut that screwed on to the barrel bushing against the flanged barrel, holding it

securely in place. This same method is used on the version described in this book.

I made up a magazine adaptor, which not only reduced the size of the magazine well to just accept a 9mm magazine (I used Sten magazines) but also served as a mounting bracket for the ejector and housed the magazine latch. A combination carrying handle and rear sight assembly was formed from sheet metal and welded in place to match a surplus M16 front sight assembly obtained from one of the surplus military parts companies that flourished at the time.

After some slight modifications and adjustments the assembled rifle, or carbine as

9mm pistol version. Made in the early 1980s.

Rifle version with folding stock from same period.

some would call it, performed quite well (well enough, in fact, that I managed to sell one to almost everyone who tried it). These were made in both 9mm and .45 caliber.

Since the bolt and recoil springs were completely housed in the upper receiver rather than extending back into the buttstock as the original parts did, these units were adaptable to folding stocks as well as pistol versions.

At that time there were several companies manufacturing lower receivers for these guns. These were intended, as now, to be used with military surplus parts to assemble AR-15 or M16 rifles. They ranged from excellent quality to pure junk. One such gun, which was equipped with a cast aluminum receiver, was accidentally knocked over onto the floor from a leaning position against the wall and broke into two parts. Naturally, I didn't use any more of these or install my parts on them. In addition, I soon discovered that dimensions varied considerably between the various brands—especially the magazine openings.

This did not actually present a problem as long as I was dealing with lower assemblies belonging to local customers. They brought them to my shop and I assembled the units, fitting the parts as required. The only trouble I experienced was with one would-be customer. This punk was a native of New York City, come down to our part of the country to enlighten us poor, ignorant

hillbillies as to how the outside world behaved. He was one of these people who talked all the time, and when he did let anyone else get in a few words he didn't hear anything they said since his mind was occupied with what he was going to say next. This guy bought several of these units from me and ruined every one of them. In spite of what I told him to the contrary, he tried everything he could think of to modify them to fire full automatic and otherwise "improve" them. I finally got all I could stand of him and ran him off. He

Full-length view showing unit mounted on Colt-made lower.

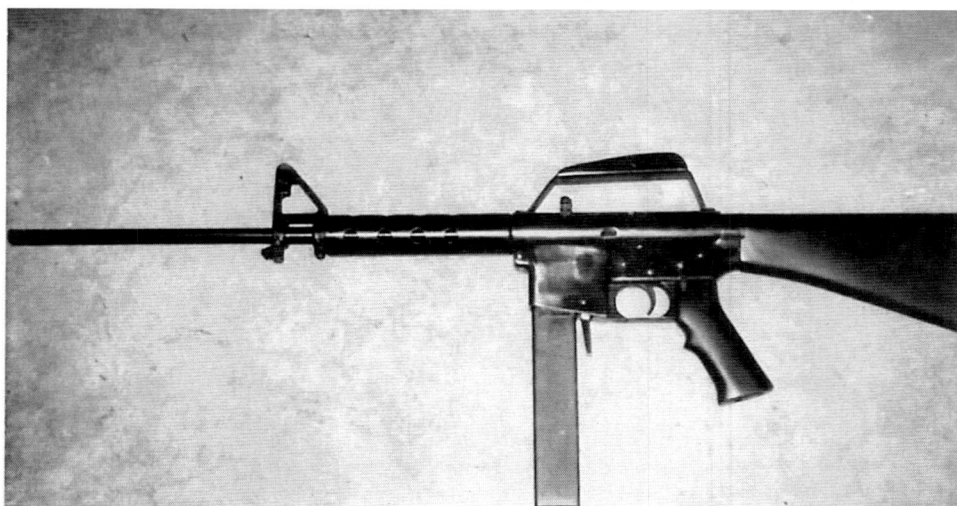

Mounted on shop-made receiver.

9mm conversion unit mounted on commercial receiver.

Same unit on shop-made lower receiver.

has ruined almost every other gun he has owned.

Finally, after the local market was satisfied, I decided to advertise the upper receiver assemblies along with a magazine adaptor and magazine in several national publications. A couple of gun magazines gave them favorable mention, and it wasn't long before a steady market was created.

About this time, though, I made a serious mistake. I neglected to take into consideration the fact that my average customer didn't bother to read my instruction sheet. I had built the magazine adaptors to fit the largest magazine wells I had encountered, and the instruction sheet that was enclosed with each unit directed the customer to reduce the width of the adaptor slightly until it was a push fit in the magazine opening, as required. I also supplied recoil springs that were slightly longer than needed, specifying that these should be cut, one coil at a time, until satisfactory functioning was obtained. The instructions also explained that the rear mounting pin hole sometimes required moving slightly.

Shortly after I began filling orders for these I got a phone call from a man in Florida. Without preamble he proceeded to call me every foul name he could think of, eventually telling me that the unit I sent him wasn't worth a damn. When I finally managed to get in a word, I asked him if he had read the instruction sheet.

"To hell with any instruction sheet," he retorted. "I'm a federally licensed gunsmith, and I don't need an instruction sheet. The damn parts don't fit."

About this time I lost my temper too, and I proceeded to inform him that possession of a federal firearms license was not an indication of either intelligence or ability. I told him that most of the names he had called me not only applied to him too, but his mother and wife as well. This got

his attention, so I told him I would send along another, slightly smaller magazine adaptor and another instruction sheet, which I insisted he read. To his credit, several days later I received a letter from him stating that he had made it work and apologizing for his previous conduct.

But such incidents happened too often. It took too much time to straighten out the problems, which were not my fault in the first place. I turned the entire operation over to a friend of mine and went on to other things.

Several years later I designed and built a few of the round-receivered versions similar to those described in this book. These were made in both 9mm and .45 versions and included the open-bolt

9mm conversion (pistol version).

pistol version described herein. This open-bolt version has interchangeable trigger parts that pivot on the same cross pins as the original parts and will fire both as a full- or semiautomatic. I made and sold several of these, but after a time—even though I was only furnishing parts—I became concerned about their legality and discontinued them as well.

Several months ago, as I prepared to put this book together, I built a new upper receiver assembly and a magazine adaptor in the rifle version that used the standard lower receiver assembly. I also built a new open-bolt pistol assembly using my own parts in the trigger mechanism as before. These were fabricated primarily for photographic purposes, to use in illustrating this book. These parts included several slight improvements (?) over the older versions and functioned quite well when attached to a standard lower receiver.

Then, just about the time I was putting the finishing touches on the book, another setback occurred. Congress passed the so-called "Crime Bill" of 1994, and suddenly lower receivers, which had been selling for $60 to $80 each, skyrocketed to an asking price of more than $400. Even worse, no more can be produced.

Realizing the problem this would cause if the time ever came when one was compelled to build such a gun or remain defenseless, I went back and designed and built a substitute lower that is made using formed sheet metal with welded-in gussets and ends. The result is actually quite a bit sturdier than the original, although heavier. It does, however, provide an alternative that will allow the builder to construct the entire gun from raw materials.

The gun, then, as described in this book, can be built as either a rifle or pistol, open or closed bolt, semi- or full automatic, and with either a self-contained bolt and recoil spring assembly or a heavier bolt that uses the original recoil spring/buffer assembly.

As things stand at present, it is likely that any version of this gun would be illegal if manufactured in its entirety. However, if the closed-bolt version of the upper receiver assembly is used with an existing lower receiver, it would probably be considered a legal gun. Just how this makes either version any more or less lethal and dangerous than the other is beyond me. But the dimwits we pay to dream up such rules seem to think that those laws will, in some fashion, reduce crime.

It is strongly recommended that readers carefully research all laws concerning building or possessing such a firearm before finishing and assembling the gun. Unfinished parts are not supposed to be illegal, but this too may change. Be careful.

MATERIALS AND TOOLS

Sheet metal, as used in this project, can usually be obtained locally. The 12-gauge material can, as a rule, be found in sheet metal shops and metal fabrication plants. If possible, try to get the type with a cold finish, commonly known as "cold rolled." This will have a bright finish as opposed to the rough black finish of the "hot rolled" type. It will cost a little more, but the time saved in finishing it will make up for it. Salvage yards are also a good source for this. If you aren't able to obtain it elsewhere, material cut from older automobile or light truck frames can be used. The biggest problem with this source is the amount of work it takes to get it. Actually, though, this could be an advantage, since the car frame contains better material than common sheet metal.

Leaf springs from cars or light trucks can be used for flat stock material, and axles from the same source will provide round stock. Valve stems salvaged from four-cycle engines, as well as shock absorber shafts, can be used for small-diameter parts. Most of this material will require annealing to soften it to a point where it can be machined easily. This can be done using a large wood fire as described in several of my other books. If a bluing setup is available, material can

A heavy vise can be used as a press brake to form sheet metal parts, among other uses.

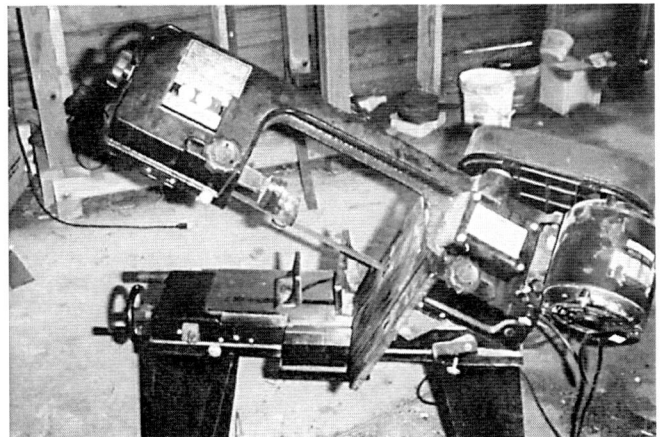

A metal-cutting band saw will save a lot of elbow grease.

1

be suspended over a bluing tank burner and heated. Actually the term "annealed" is a misnomer as used here, since the hardened material can be made workable by heating it to a temperature of 800 to 1,000 degrees and allowing it to cool slowly.

4130 seamless tubing, as used here, can be ordered from the following supplier:

Wicks Aircraft Supply
410 Pine St.
Highland, IL 62249

This is the best source of supply for not only the tubing but also 4130 and 4340 round stock, as well as flat stock of the same material. Not only are they a source for all of the heat-treatable steel required, but these are nice people. Anyone who has dealt with large, arrogant steel companies who don't really want to deal in small amounts of material anyway will appreciate this. Another plus is that they will ship by UPS, COD, usually within 24 hours of the time the order is received.

Coil springs are available from automotive supply houses and hardware stores.

Leaf springs are the source of heat-treatable flat stock.

Material to be softened is placed in wood pile.

Wood fire will soften hard steel, making it workable.

Softened steel is removed from ashes after cooling.

Round stock is available from many sources.

Sten magazines are still available at a reasonable price from the following source:

Manchester Arms
P.O. Box 129
Lenoir City, TN 37771

Even before the assault weapons bill went into effect, most suppliers of these and other surplus parts raised their prices to exorbitant levels with the mistaken idea that there would be such a demand for these that customers would pay the price. The owner of Manchester Arms, told me recently that she still has some 10,000 Sten magazines on hand. Her price is $4 each for new magazines and $2 each for used. You might want to order a magazine loading tool at the same time. These make loading the magazines considerably easier.

Barrel blanks are available from a number of sources. Most are satisfactory. For some 20 years now I have obtained most of my barrels from the following supplier:

E. R. Shaw
Thoms Run Road and Presley
Bridgeville, PA 15017
These barrels are fully as good as most that I

have had experience with and far better than some. And, like most people I deal with a second time, the folks at E.R. Shaw are decent, helpful people (unlike some of the arrogant smart alecks at some of the other companies, who seem to feel that they are doing you a favor if they condescend to sell you something).

Small parts, such as the M1 carbine recoil springs, hammer springs, hammers, triggers, firing pins, and so on, are available from the following source:

Quality Parts Co.
P.O. Box 1479
Roosevelt Trail #3
Windham, ME 04062

The people at Quality Parts also build the Bushmaster versions of the M16 and have built and sold complete firearms to the military. Their parts, like their complete guns, are top quality. They sell only new parts, but usually for less money than most of the salvage shysters want for worn out junk.

A lathe is required to build this gun.

This welder is capable of MIG, TIG, and stick welding modes.

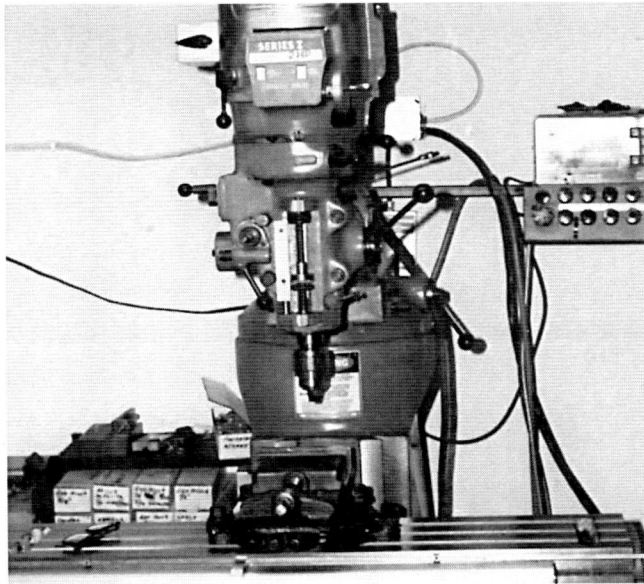

A milling machine will save a lot of hand work, although most operations required here can be done using files, saws, chisels, and grinder.

Chamber reamers are available from the following source:

Clymer Mfg. Co.
1645 W. Hamlin Road
Rochester Hills, MI 48309

Here again, I have used these chamber reamers ever since the company has been in business, and even before when it was owned by other people. There are none better for our purpose.

No doubt there are other suppliers who provide equal quality, courtesy, and dependability. My endorsement of those listed here is not intended as a slight to anyone else. (Well, almost anyone else.) My experience with those listed has been satisfying enough that I simply never bothered to look anywhere else.

Several of my other books include fairly thorough discussions of tools and equipment, and they need not be repeated here. This project requires some lathe and mill work, as well as a small amount of welding. The rest can be done with hand tools if absolutely necessary.

This gas welding set is used for silver-soldering, heat-treating, and coloring operations.

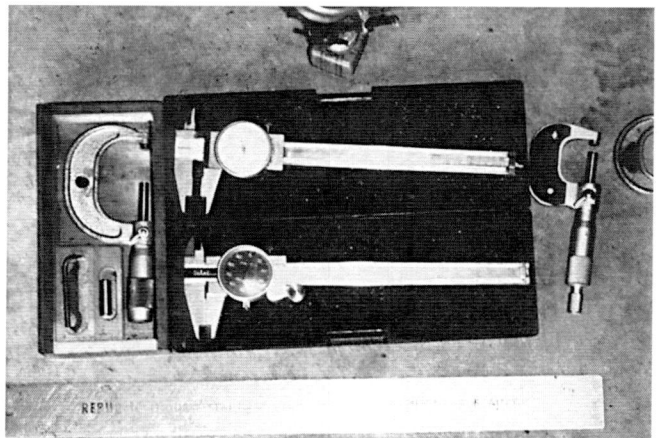

Several measuring tools will come in handy.

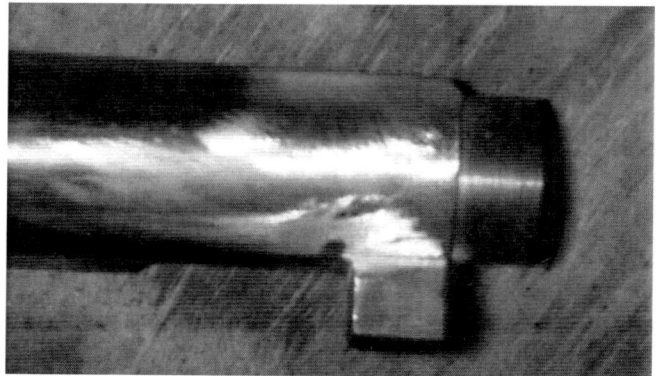

Welds are dressed flush with the surface.

A large (3/4 to 1 hp) electric motor equipped with an arbor can drive buffing wheels, sanding discs, etc.

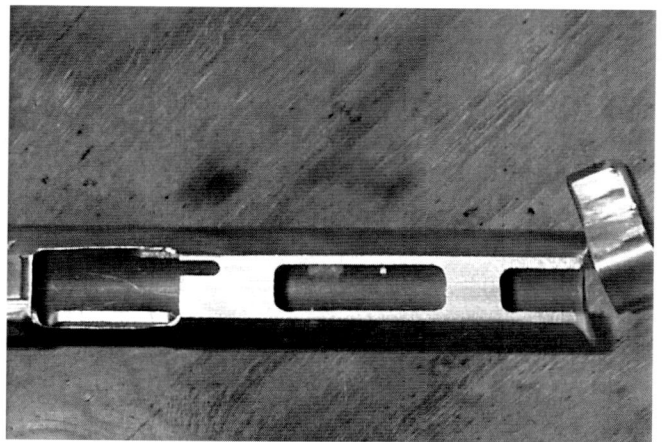

Various openings are formed as required.

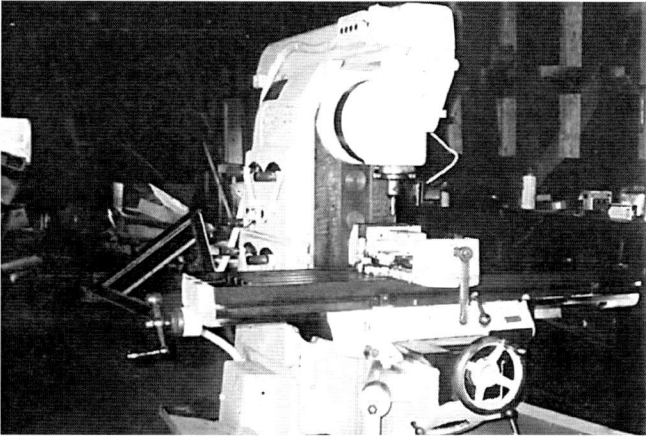

Older horizontal/vertical milling machines can often be obtained quite cheaply. Most are still accurate and offer good value.

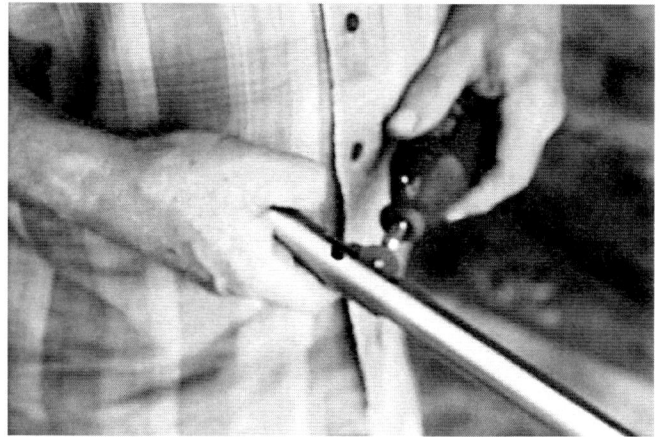

Small high-speed grinders will do many of the milling machine operations.

I have learned recently that several different machine tool importers are presently marketing a fairly compact combination lathe, milling machine, and drill press. While most of these are apparently made in the same place and have a common design with different brand names affixed, the best appears to be one called a "Smithy." This is primarily because it has a hole through the spindle that is quite a bit larger than the others. This will allow the would-be gun builder to chuck the barrel and chamber and thread them up close to the head stock with the bulk of the barrel extending through the spindle. This brand also has a longer cross slide (which does double duty as a milling table) than the other brands I have seen. One of these machines—if they are any good—would be relatively inexpensive and require only a small amount of space. I intend to obtain one in the near future for use in preparation of a book on home workshop survival weapons. Stay tuned.

Please note that the suppliers listed here were in business at the addresses listed when this book was published, and since they are all stable companies, I assume that they still are. Please don't complain to me or the publisher if this has changed.

UPPER RECEIVER

The upper receiver, being essentially the same for both the rifle and pistol versions, is made from 1 1/2-inch-outside-diameter seamless tubing with a wall thickness of .120 inch. This is a standard size, available from most metal supply houses. It can also be obtained from aircraft building materials suppliers, several of which cater to builders of home-built aircraft. These are probably better sources, since they will usually sell it in short lengths, whereas the metal supply houses want to sell full-length sticks measuring 20 feet or more.

High strength is not a requirement for the material used in this receiver since little stress is present in use. Although cheaper grades of tubing are available, I would still use the tubing made of 4130 if possible. It is tougher than the cheaper grades and will resist wear better. It is also more suitable for welding than the cheaper grades.

Construction is begun by cutting the receiver body to length and squaring both ends. Four 1/4-inch or slightly larger holes are drilled just behind the front face and spaced equally around the circumference of the receiver. A plug, which will serve as a barrel bushing, is turned to a diameter that will just slip into the

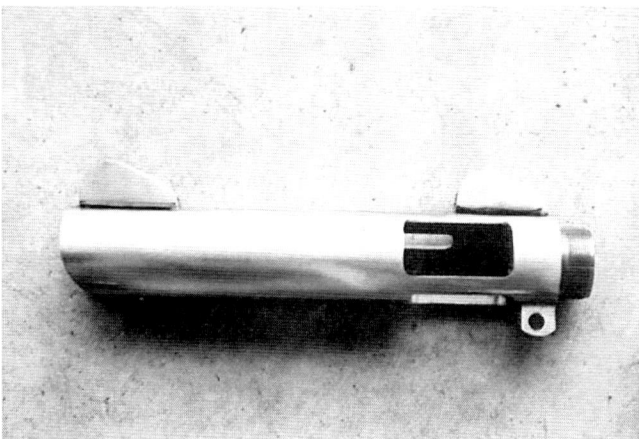

Upper receiver ready for polishing (right side).

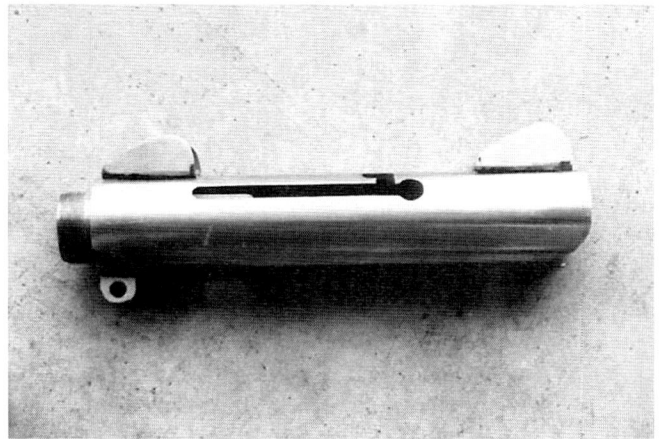

Upper receiver (left side).

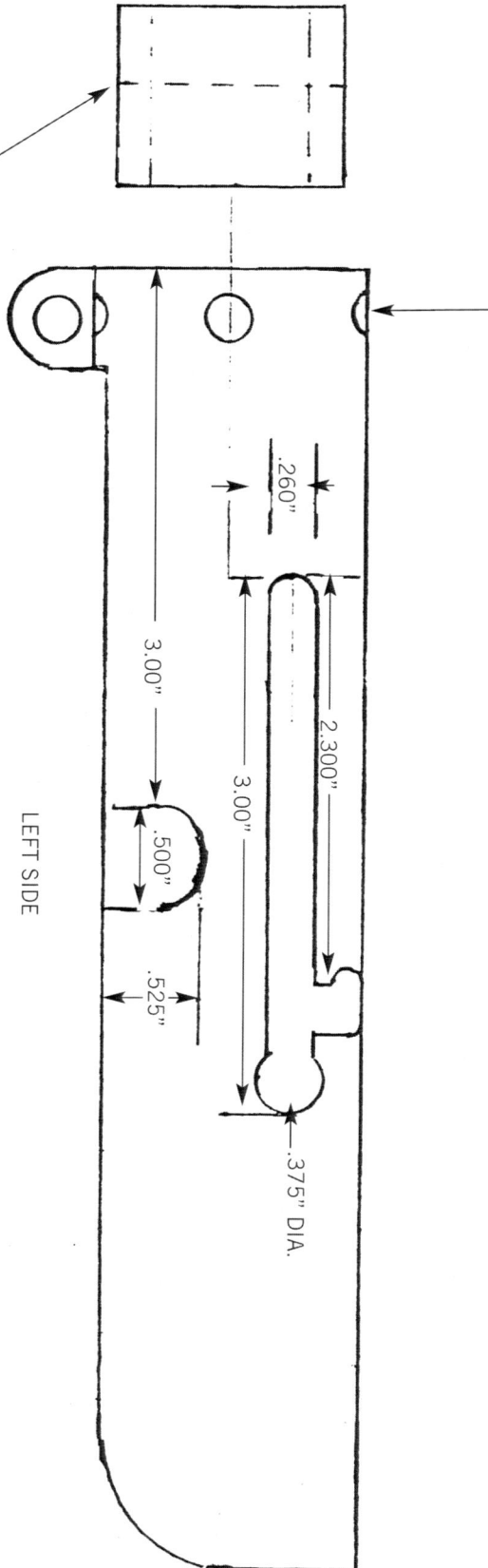

UPPER RECEIVER

LEFT SIDE

.260"

3.00"

2.300"

3.00"

.500"

.525"

.375" DIA.

FOUR .250" DIAMETER HOLES DRILLED EQUADISTANTLY AROUND CIRCUMFERENCE OF RECEIVER. BARREL BUSHING IS WELDED IN PLACE THROUGH THESE.

BARREL BUSHING 1.100" LONG. TURNED TO CLOSE FIT INSIDE RECEIVER.

Diagram #1

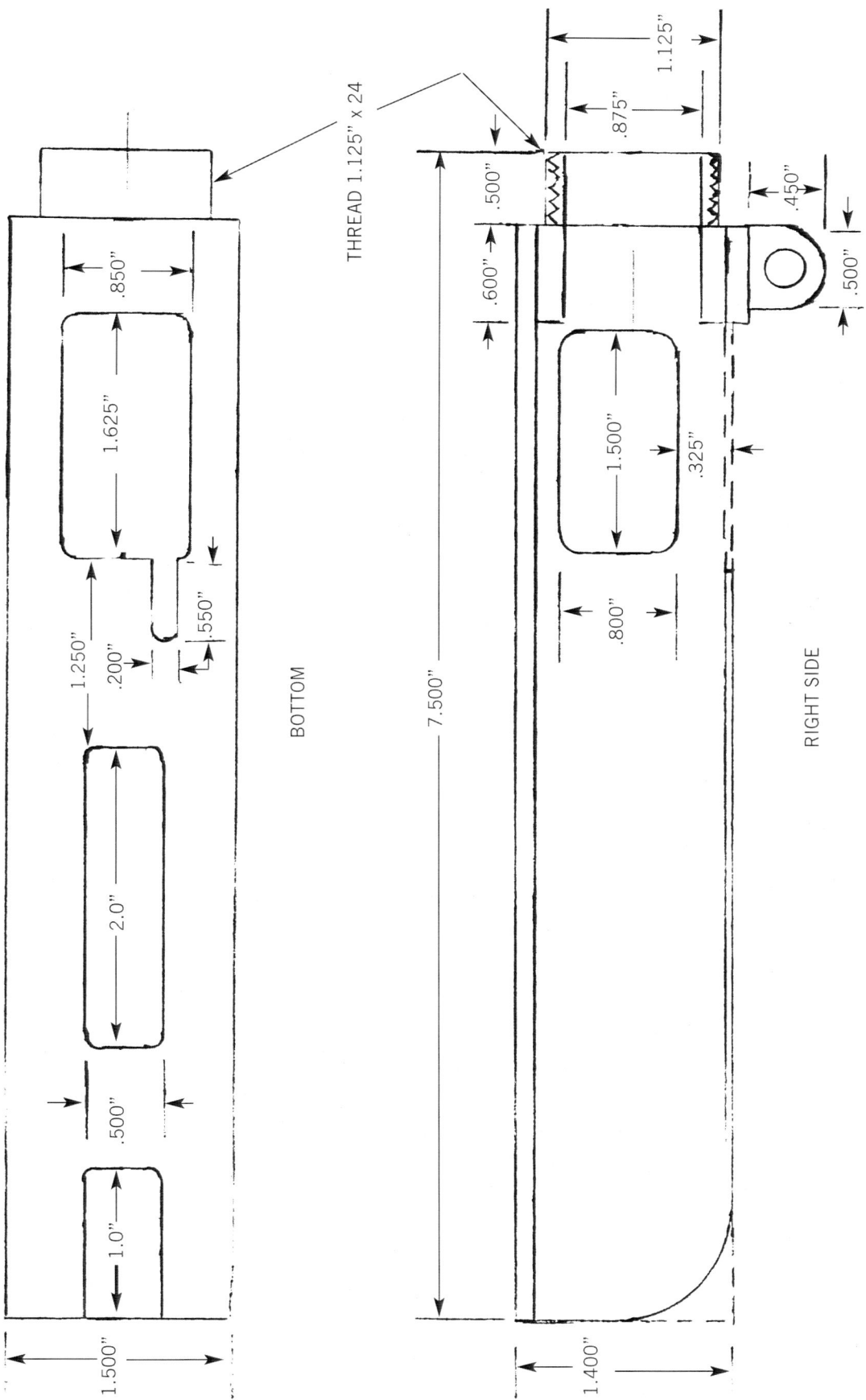

THREAD 1.125" x 24

.850"

1.625"

1.250"

.200"

.550"

1.0"

.500"

2.0"

1.500"

BOTTOM

1.125"

.875"

.500"

.600"

.450"

.500"

7.500"

1.500"

.325"

.800"

1.400"

RIGHT SIDE

UPPER RECEIVER

Diagram #2

11

front end of the receiver. One-and-a-quarter-inch material is slightly small for this since the inside of the receiver measures 1.260 inches. So slightly larger material should be turned to fit. While the hole through the bushing will have a finished diameter of .875 inch, it should be kept smaller and bored to size after the bushing is welded in place. The bushing should be positioned inside the receiver with .600 inch extending back into the receiver and secured permanently in place by welding through the four holes and building the welds up above the surface far enough that they can be dressed back flush. TIG welding is ideal for this. If this is done properly, no trace of the welds will show.

A cube of steel 1/2" x 1/2" x 1/2" is likewise welded in place on what will be the exact bottom center of the receiver blank. It should be relieved on all four sides where it joins the receiver and built back up above the surface with weld material and machined back flush. The forward edge should be flush with the receiver face.

The assembly is now chucked in the lathe and the barrel bushing bored to .875 inch. There should be .500 inch of the bushing extending past the front face of the receiver. This is turned to a diameter of 1.125 inches and threaded 24 threads per inch.

For both receivers to mate properly and the inside diameters of both the upper receiver and the lower receiver spring tube to be concentric and parallel, .100 inch of material must be removed from the exact bottom side of the upper receiver. The centerline of the front hinge block is used as a reference point and the flat machined as indicated. This is best done with the milling machine, using a face mill or other large-diameter end mill. The radius at the bottom rear should be cut to match the contour of the lower receiver as closely as possible. This can be accomplished in several ways. Probably the easiest way is through use of a rotary table in the milling machine. Another way is through use of a radius-cutting—or corner-rounding, as some call them—end mill. In lieu of either of these, it can be formed by hand using a disc sander. If care is used and the fit is checked frequently, this method will achieve the same result as the others. It will just take longer.

Barrel bushing and front hinge block are welded in place.

Welding completed.

Whichever method is used, when the fit is as close as possible, both receivers should be clamped together and the front hinge pin hole drilled.

Before the hole is drilled, however, a bushing is turned to fit the lower receiver front hinge pin hole closely, and a 1/8-inch hole is drilled through the center. This bushing is placed in the front hinge pin hole of the lower receiver, and the hole is drilled through the upper receiver hinge block using a 1/8-inch drill. The receivers are then separated and the hole enlarged to full size using a 1/4-inch drill. The purpose of the drill bushing is to protect the soft aluminum lower receiver from damage caused by use of a full-size drill or

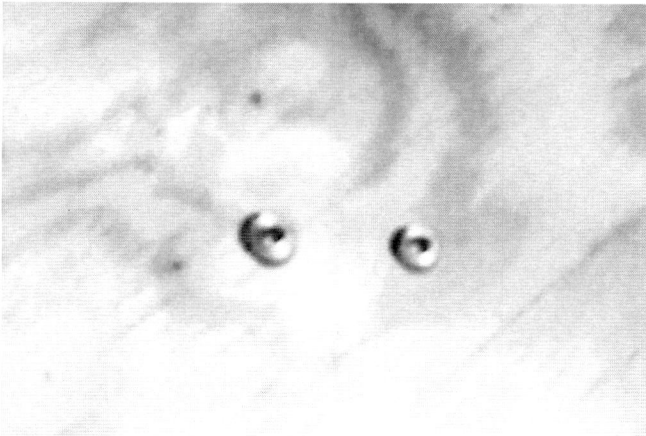

Drill bushings.

Drilling front hinge-pin hole.

Shop-built upper, clamped to commercial lower with bushing in front pin hole, ready for drilling.

Pistol upper unit, ready for mounting.

mutilation from metal chips or shavings.

If the shop-made steel receiver pictured in the Preface is used, the drill bushing is not necessary since the hole is drilled through both receivers simultaneously.

If a new commercial receiver or the shop-made receiver is used, or if you have means to remove the recoil spring tube from your existing receiver, a better fit can sometimes be obtained by turning a close-fitting mandrel to fit inside the upper receiver and using a cap and drawbolt to pull it back tightly against the lower receiver at the rear end before clamping and drilling. With the cross pin in place, the upper receiver assembly should swivel from the closed position to almost a right angle. The bottom, front, and rear of the mounting block must be shaped to a half round configuration to permit this.

A bracket to accept the rear mounting cross pin is made by welding a 1/2-inch steel cube to the outside surface of a section of 1 1/4-inch-outside-diameter tubing. This should have a wall thickness of .065 inch and a length of .625 inch to .650 inch. The side of the cube adjacent to the tubing should be radiused to fit the tubing closely with the sides and ends angled. The seam, or joint, is built back above the surface by welding. The weld joints are then dressed back flush with the surface and the block width reduced to .475 inch.

13

REAR MOUNTING BRACKET

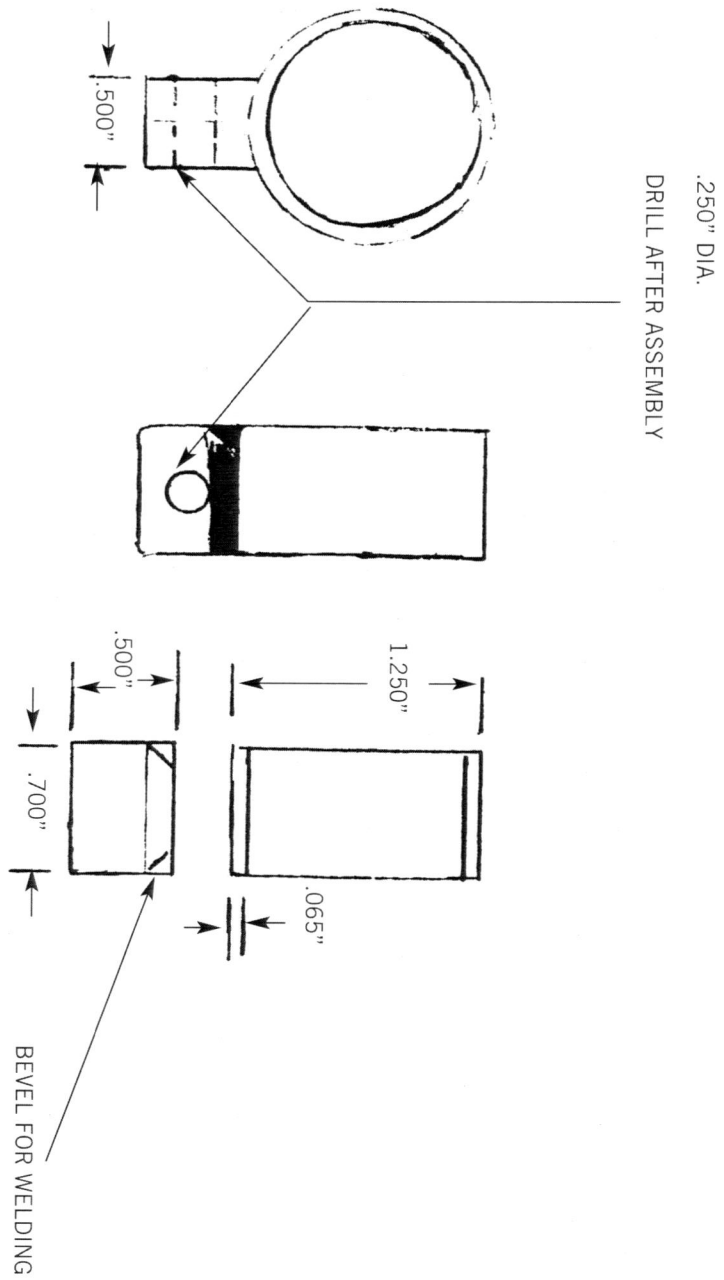

.500"

.250" DIA.
DRILL AFTER ASSEMBLY

.500"

.700"

1.250"

.065"

BEVEL FOR WELDING

Diagram #3

Cut near center to clear bolt release.

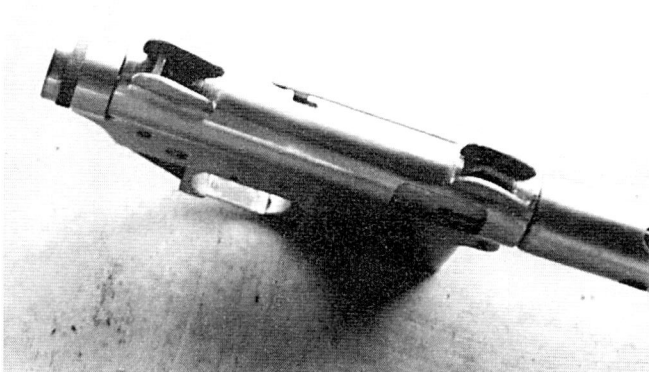

Completed receiver assembly.

Upper receiver with rear mounting bracket in place.

A slot to accept this block is cut at the bottom rear of the upper receiver to the dimensions shown in Diagram #2. The slot to clear the hammer can also be cut at this time, as well as the magazine opening, including a slot to provide clearance for the ejector.

If a commercial lower receiver is used, either a relief cut must be made in the left side of the upper receiver to clear the bolt-hold-open release button or the bolt-hold-open device must be removed. This cut can be located by measuring back from the front face of the receiver as shown in Diagram #1. A simpler method, however, is to position both receivers in their respective assembled positions and mark around the hold-open button. The relief cut is not necessary if the shop-made receiver is used. Since the 9mm magazine does not extend to the rear far enough to activate the bolt-hold-open, there is no point in putting it in the receiver.

With the completed bracket and the front hinge pin in place, both receivers are clamped together, and, using the bushing as before, the mounting pin hole is drilled. Again, the drill bushing is required only if the commercial aluminum receiver is used. As with the front hole, both receivers are drilled together when using the shop-made receiver. With both pins then in place, a close-fitting assembly without any shake or play should result.

15

Slot is cut for barrel-positioning pin.

An ejection port is machined in the right side, as shown in Diagram #2. There are people who will insist that this port need not be nearly as big as the one shown. They will tell you that it is easier for dirt and debris to get into the large port. They do not tell you that it is also easier for dirt and debris to get out of the large port. There is also less chance of empty cases striking the edges of the larger port and falling back in the action, causing the gun to jam. This has happened on numerous occasions with small ejection ports. Make your choice.

The lengthwise slot, to accommodate the cocking lever, or charging handle, is cut in the left side in a 10:30 o'clock, or 315°, position (45° above the centerline) when viewed from the rear. The "dog leg" at the upper rear serves as a safety in the open-bolt version. Although it is not required for the closed bolt, it will serve as a bolt-hold-open if included.

A 1/8-inch-wide slot, .200 inch long, must be cut beginning at the front face of the threaded barrel bushing and on the top centerline. The locating pin on the breech end of the barrel fits into this and keeps the barrel located in its correct position.

BOLT

While three different bolt assemblies are shown in the following diagrams, they have a common configuration as far as the size and shape of the magazine cuts, the bolt nose, and the extractor cuts. One version is for use in the open-bolt gun and has a fixed integral firing pin. Another, which is the same length and diameter, is intended to be contained entirely inside the receiver, making possible a closed-bolt pistol version. The third is a full-length bolt intended for use with the original recoil spring and buffer. This is the one to use if the unit is to be interchanged with the original .223 upper receiver assembly.

Even though several of the dimensions are the same for all three, we will discuss the construction details of each one separately. This will entail some repetition but may also avoid confusion.

OPEN BOLT

The open-bolt version should be cut to length with both ends squared. A bolt nose is turned on one end of the bolt body. This should extend .150 inch forward from the bolt body proper and have an outside diameter of .550 inch if used as a 9mm. The .45 version should be .650 inch. A counterbore slightly larger than the cartridge head is cut .100 inch deep. This should have an inside diameter of .400 inch for the 9mm or .480 inch for the .45. In the center of this, a fixed firing pin, .060 inch in diameter, is formed. This should have a hemispherical point and protrude .050 inch from the bolt face. A fairly simple way to form this is to chuck an open-center, or non-center-cutting 3/8-inch end mill, in the lathe tail stock drill chuck. With the bolt turning in the headstock chuck, the end mill is fed into the bolt face with the tail stock. This will form the inside diameter some .020 inch to .025 inch undersize

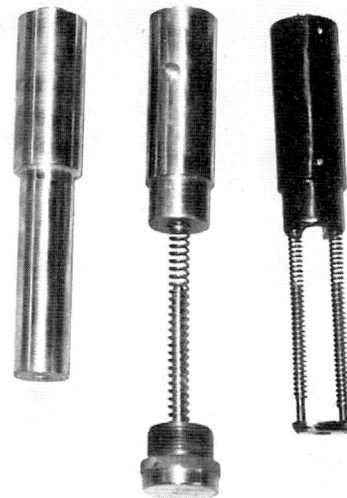

From left: full-length bolt, open-bolt assembly, closed-bolt assembly.

17

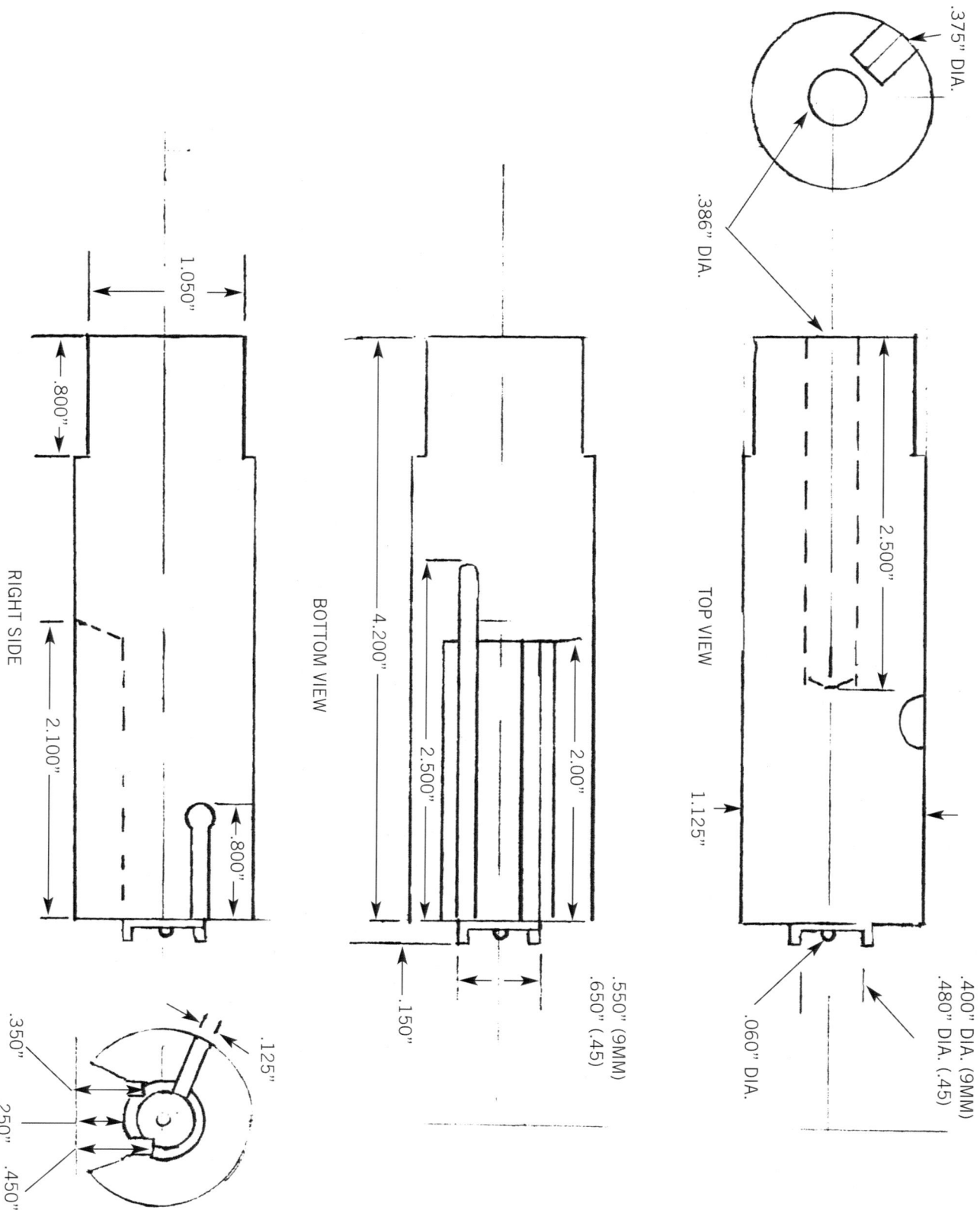

.375" DIA.

.386" DIA.

TOP VIEW

2.500"

1.125"

.400" DIA. (9MM)
.480" DIA. (.45)

.060" DIA.

1.050"

.800"

OPEN BOLT

RIGHT SIDE

2.100"

.800"

BOTTOM VIEW

4.200"

2.500"

2.00"

.150"

.550" (9MM)
.650" (.45)

.350"

.125"

.250"

.450"

Diagram #4

End view showing bolt nose configuration.

Magazine clearance is cut with end mill.

in the case of the 9mm, and the open center of the milling cutter will leave a small projection that can be turned to form the firing pin using a lathe cutting tool ground to form it. The outside cutting edge of this same tool is used to bring the counterbore to the correct diameter.

With this accomplished, the bolt is reversed in the lathe chuck, whereupon a hole of sufficient size to accept the recoil spring is drilled, as shown in Diagram #4. The hole diameter should be slightly larger than the spring used to assure free movement of the spring as it compresses.

In the prototype gun, the spring used measured .375 inch in diameter. The hole was drilled with a "W" drill measuring .386 inch in diameter. A 25/64 drill, which measures .3906 inch, would be equally satisfactory. A slight bevel should be formed at the entrance of the hole, which will assist in reducing friction and binding.

While the bolt is chucked in this position, the rear end of the body can be reduced in diameter as shown in the diagram. This is required to allow the bolt to travel entirely to the rear of the receiver, with the smaller-diameter portion moving freely inside the rear mounting bracket.

The bolt is now secured in the milling machine vise and a slot cut down the exact center

using a 5/8-inch end mill. The slot should be cut to a depth that just meets the outside diameter of the bolt nose and a length of 2.250 inches. Upon completion of this, a deeper slot is cut along each side of the cavity using a 1/8-inch end mill. These are to provide clearance for the magazine lips and the ejector. The slot on the extractor side should be cut to a depth slightly less than that of the inside counterbore. The other side must be cut approximately .100 inch deeper to clear the extractor. Properly done, this will leave a strip 1/4 inch wide that is the same depth as the bottom of the bolt nose. These slots must be cut long enough to clear the back side of the magazine on the one side and the rear of the extractor on the other. Next the bolt is rotated 15 degrees and a cut made down the side. It is then rotated back 30 degrees in the other direction and a matching cut made. These will closely match the magazine sides while providing ample clearance between the bolt and magazine.

The extractor cut is made with a 1/8-inch end mill in a ten o'clock position when viewed from the front. The slot should be cut to the inside edge of the bolt nose counterbore. A spring pocket is cut to the same depth at the extreme rear end of the slot using a 3/16-inch end mill.

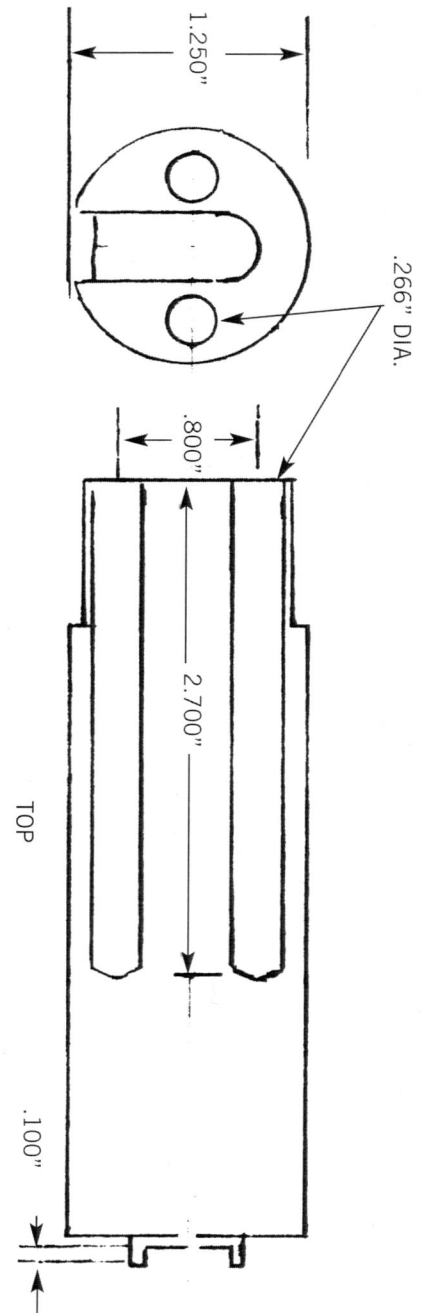

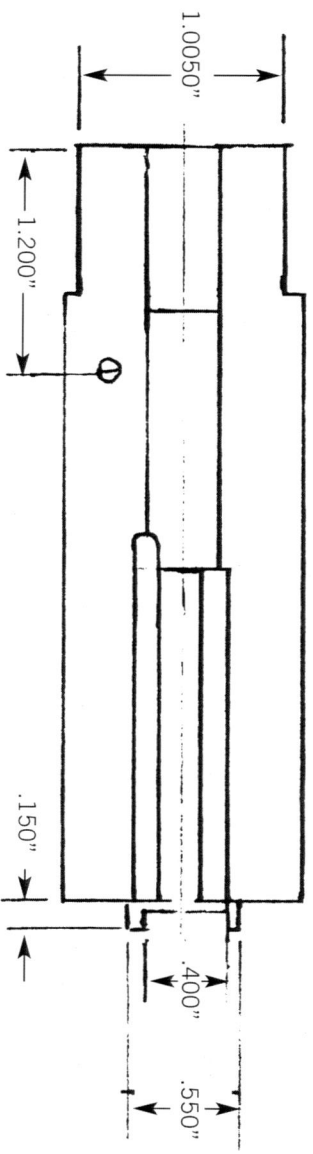

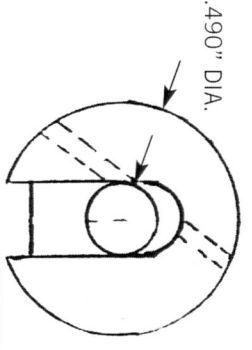

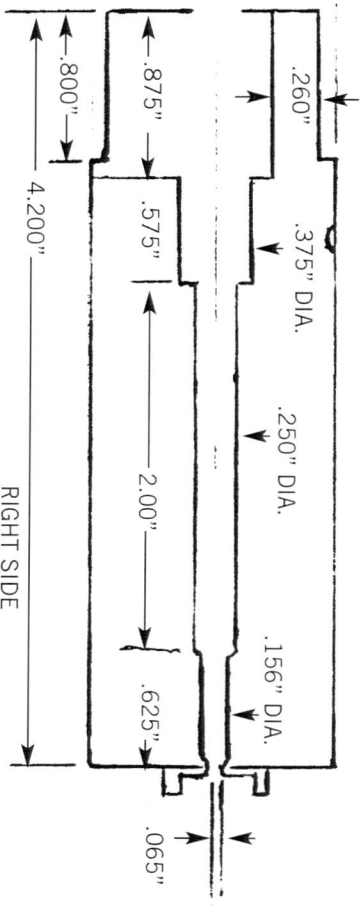

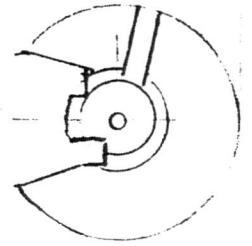

.490" DIA.

1.250"

.266" DIA.

.800"

2.700"

TOP

1.0050"

1.200"

BOTTOM

.150"

400"

.550"

.800"

.875"

.260"

.575"

.375" DIA.

.250" DIA.

2.00"

.156" DIA.

.625"

4.200"

.065"

.100"

CLOSED BOLT

RIGHT SIDE

Diagram #5

20

Open bolt (left) shows fixed firing pin. Closed bolt (right) shows firing pin hole.

CLOSED BOLT

The short closed bolt is made in the same manner and to the same outside dimensions, except that instead of the fixed firing pin, a .070-inch hole is drilled in the center of the bolt counterbore. A No. 50 drill is correct for this. Before the counterbore is cut, this hole should be started with a center drill, fed by the tail stock chuck. The drill is then used to drill the small hole approximately 1/2 inch deep. The exact depth doesn't matter since a larger hole, drilled from the opposite end, will enlarge most of it. This small drill should be withdrawn and cleaned frequently, and amply lubricated. Otherwise it may very well seize and break off in the hole. If this should happen, you might as well get another piece of material and start over, since that would prove far easier than getting the broken drill out.

The counterbore can now be cut to its full depth and diameter, removing any trace of the oversized hole made by the center drill.

Since the firing-pin design used in the original bolt would be hard to improve on, we will use it in our bolt. A surplus military firing pin should be acquired before the bolt is machined to accept it. These are plentiful at present, and at a good price. If none are available, one can be lathe turned using the dimensions and directions shown in the Small Parts chapter (Diagram #42). The bolt body is reversed in the lathe chuck and, starting the hole with a center drill, an opening to accept the firing pin is made. This opening will consist of three diameters, four if the firing pin hole nose hole already drilled is counted. Start by drilling with a 1/4-inch drill to a depth of 3 inches. This depth need not be exact, but close approximation should be kept. This is followed by drilling with a 3/8-inch drill to a depth slightly less than 1.450 inches.

This portion requires a square, or flat, shoulder at the bottom. It can be formed by using a 3/8-inch end mill to reach the final depth. This should be as close to the previously mentioned depth of 1.450 inches as possible. A smaller hole, .120 inch in diameter, extends from the bottom of the 1/4-inch-diameter portion to a point just behind the bolt face. This should have a total depth of 4 inches. Since ordinary twist drills of sufficient length are not normally available from hardware stores and the like, and even those obtained through special order are limber and subject to easy breakage, we can make up a suitable drill for this purpose fairly easily.

Chuck a piece of 1/4-inch drill rod that is at least 4 inches long (7 inches if you ever intend to make up the full-length bolt described next) and, using the tail stock chuck, drill a hole in one end using a No. 31 drill. This, of course, is started with a center drill, which by now should be standard practice. The drill is then reversed and, with a small amount of flux applied, pushed into the hole just drilled and silver-soldered in place. The end of the drill protruding from the drill rod (it should protrude at least 1 inch) must be protected from the heat used to silver-solder it in place to prevent drawing the temper. It will likely be necessary to polish the larger 1/4-inch section where it was heated before it will enter the hole freely. The depth of these holes can be regulated closely through the use of stops made by fastening close-fitting collars around the drill stems, or extensions, with the exact length to drill the holes extending. Such collars can be fastened in place with solder or epoxy.

This bolt design requires two small-diameter recoil springs located on either side of the firing pin. The recoil springs used in the military M1 carbine are well suited for this. They are plentiful and cheap. The diameter of these is approximately .260 inch. The holes to accept these should be slightly larger for clearance. A 17/64-inch drill, which measures .2656 inch, will serve well for this. These holes should be 2.700 inches deep and measure .800 inch apart from center to center with .400 inch on each side of the centerline.

A slot must be cut, as shown in the drawing, to permit the hammer to move forward far enough to contact the firing pin. This is done by clamping the bolt in a vertical position in the milling machine and cutting it with a 3/8-inch end mill. This slot should be .875 inch deep, provided that the overall length of 4.200 inches is adhered to. This will provide a shoulder so that when the hammer is fully forward the firing pin will protrude .050 inch through the bolt face. The distance from the extreme front of the bolt nose to this shoulder should be 3.325 inches. Firing pin protrusion can be checked and verified by pushing the firing pin forward—preferably with the return spring in place—flush with the shoulder and measuring the protrusion with a depth micrometer.

At the location shown in Diagram #5, a crosswise hole is drilled for a pin to keep the firing pin in place. A close-fitting plug should be inserted in the firing pin hole while this hole is drilled to provide support for the drill. Otherwise the drill will "creep" or "crawl" toward the unsupported side and almost certainly break.

Lower side view of both bolts.

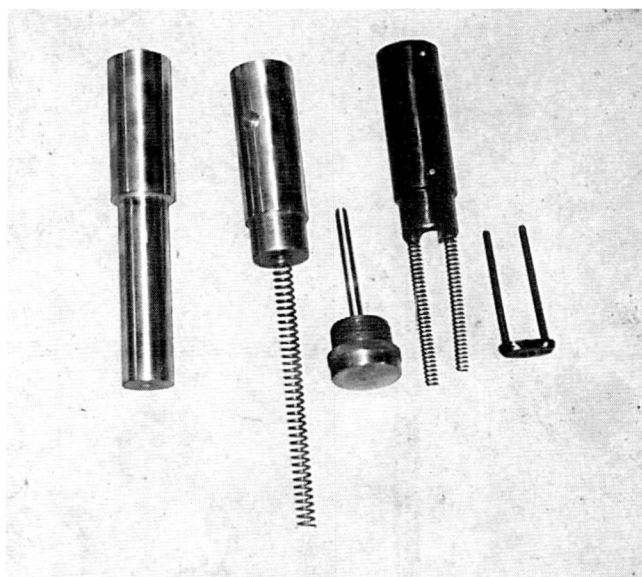

Bolt assemblies showing springs and spring guides.

Open bolt on left; closed bolt on right.

Rear view of open bolt (left) and closed bolt (right).

FULL LENGTH

The full-length bolt, which is to be used with the original recoil spring, is made in the same manner except that in this case it will have an overall length of 6.950 inches. The rear portion, measuring 3.750 inches long, is turned to a diameter of .990 inch. This assures that it will slide, without binding, inside the spring housing.

This time, the hammer slot must be cut as shown in Diagram #6, with a flat shoulder 3.325 inches to the rear of the bolt's forward face, as before, and of sufficient length to allow the hammer to travel forward and back without interference. While not actually necessary, it is easier to cut this slot all the way through the bolt body from top to bottom than the partial depth required.

The extractor pin holes are in the same location on all three versions and should be drilled with the extractor clamped in place to ensure that they line up exactly.

The cocking lever, or operating handle, is also of the same dimensions and in the same location on all three versions. The correct location for the hole in the bolt is fixed by marking its location through the receiver slot with the bolt in place and in the closed position. The operating handle must not contact the front of the slot. If possible, this hole should be drilled in the milling machine with a slightly undersized drill and finished with a 3/8-inch end mill, forming a flat bottom in the hole.

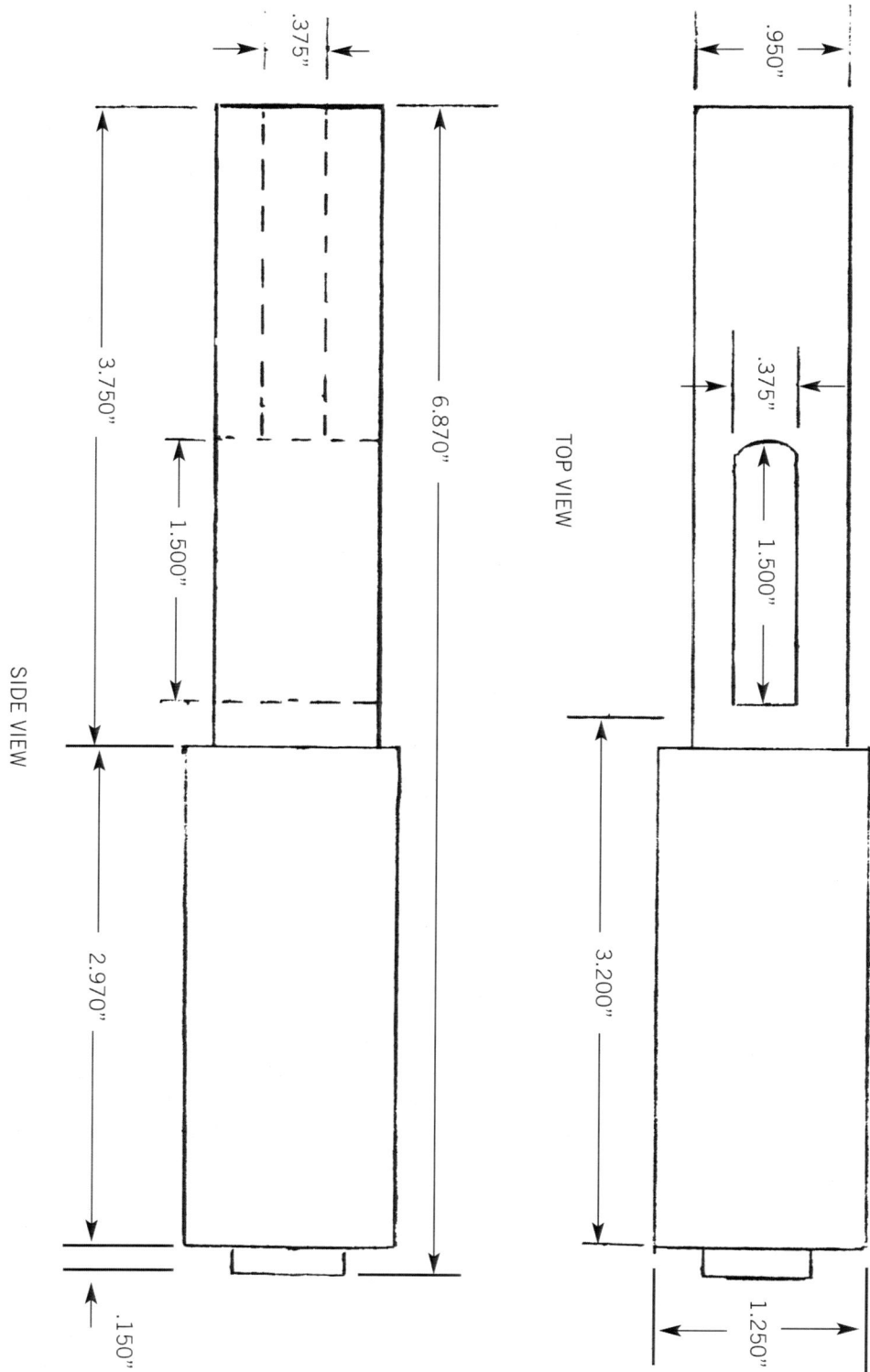

FULL-LENGTH BOLT

TOP VIEW

SIDE VIEW

.950"

.375"

1.500"

3.200"

1.250"

.375"

3.750"

1.500"

6.870"

2.970"

.150"

Diagram #6

BARREL

The barrel(s) used in this project require a retaining ring measuring 1 inch in diameter. Therefore a barrel blank with a minimum diameter of 1 inch must be used. At present, a number of barrel manufacturers offer suitable barrel blanks for this. Most, in fact, offer such blanks with a 1-inch diameter and a length of 24 inches. Since these usually come slightly longer than the advertised length, it is possible to cut four full 6-inch-length pistol barrels from one of these—even after allowing for saw cuts and squaring the ends. We can also get both a 6-inch pistol barrel and an 18-inch rifle barrel from one such blank.

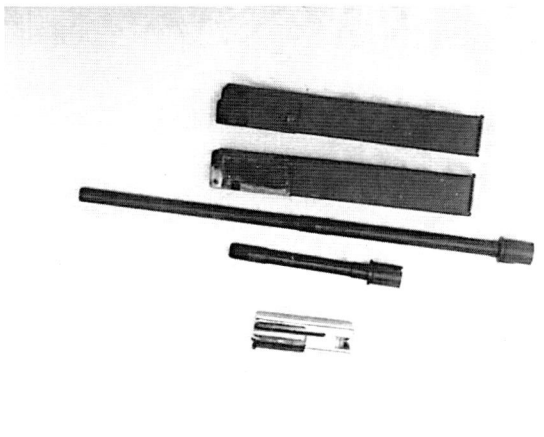

The pistol barrel can be of whatever length you choose. Although Diagram #7 shows my personal preference of a 6-inch barrel, there is no good reason why yours should not be longer or shorter if you so desire. I have always thought a 6-inch barrel has a more balanced look than other lengths.

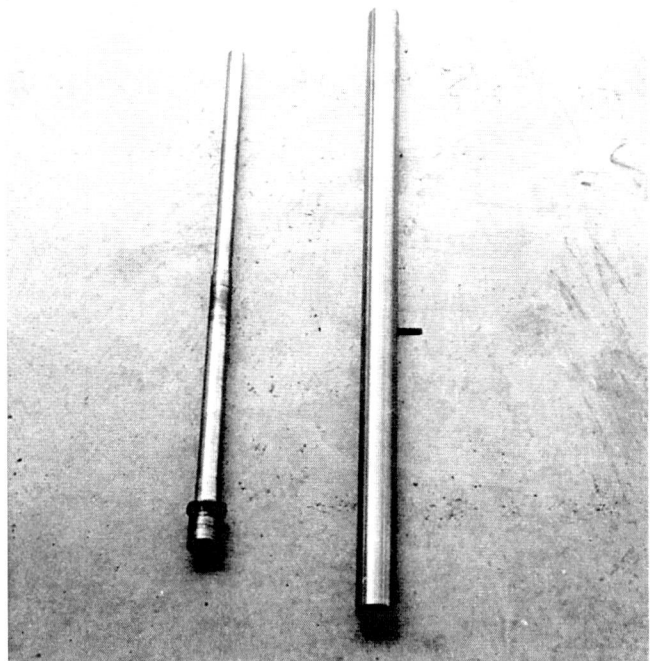

Rifle and pistol barrels made up several years ago for square receiver model but interchangeable.

Rifle barrel shown with unturned blank.

Barrel is turned to desired diameter.

End turned to length, squared.

The rifle barrel, though, is required by federal law to have a minimum length of 16 inches. Our barrel should be made slightly longer than the minimum length, simply to assure that even the stupidest law enforcement agent will be convinced that it is of legal length.

It has long been accepted by the more intelligent authorities that if a rod is inserted in the muzzle end of a barrel and pushed in until it contacts the bolt face, this length will be accepted as the barrel length. There are, however, any number of idiots that have never learned this. In fact, I can remember an instance where a stupid small-town marshal thought he was going to confiscate a shotgun of my manufacture, which I was displaying at a gun show, because the barrel only measured something over 17 inches from the muzzle to the point where it entered the receiver. Never mind the fact, which I tried to explain to him, that there was another inch of barrel extending back into the receiver. It was too short and subject to confiscation, or so he said. Luckily, a state trooper (these are usually considerably smarter than other law enforcement officers, at least in this part of the country) happened by and straightened him out. But I could have had to go to considerable trouble to get my gun back. This example should serve to illustrate the convenience of a slightly longer barrel. The one shown in the diagram is 16 1/2 inches overall, mainly because this was the length of

my barrel blank. Eighteen inches would have been more desirable.

Threaded muzzle ends, to accept muzzle brakes, flash hiders, and the like, may also be determined to be illegal. (Some of the same people mentioned above will think you intend to mount a silencer if the muzzle is threaded.) If such devices are used, they should be fastened in place permanently—preferably by pinning or silver-soldering. Bayonet lugs are also of questionable legality and should be avoided.

You will also need a way to cut the chamber. At present a number of companies manufacture and sell chamber reamers in almost any caliber one could wish for. These usually range in price from $40 to $100. Since the straight-cased pistol calibers required in this project use chambers that are only slightly larger than the bore, and only a small amount of metal is removed when cutting the chamber, only a finish reamer will be necessary. When larger bottlenecked cases are used, it is a good idea to remove the bulk of the chamber metal with a roughing reamer, which will cut the chamber slightly undersize, and follow it with the finish reamer. This is done primarily to prolong the useful life of the finish reamer. Be sure to specify that the reamer will be used in a rifle barrel when ordering it. A good many reamers for pistol calibers are made with the pilot ground to groove diameter or slightly larger for use in revolver cylinders. These will not enter the bore of the rifled barrel, which requires

.600" TO .625"

.125" BARREL INDEXING PIN

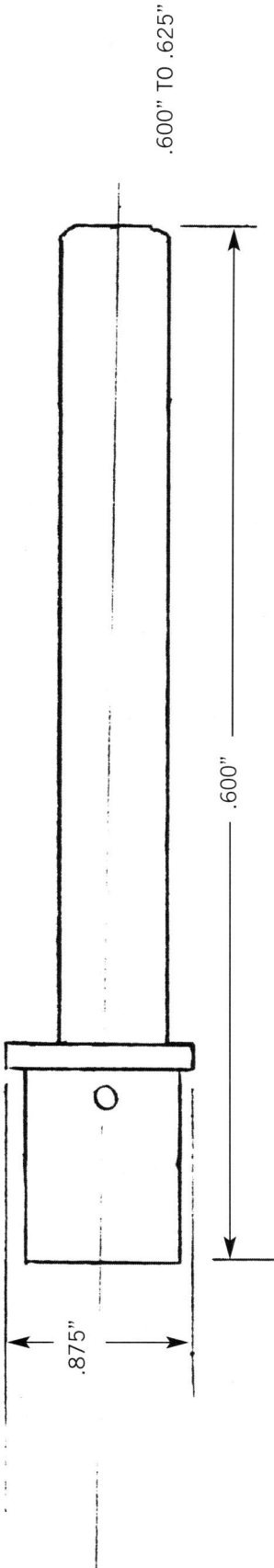

.600"

PISTOL BARREL

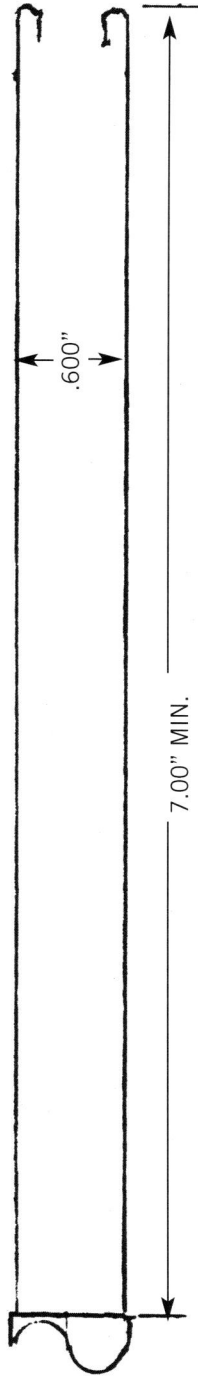

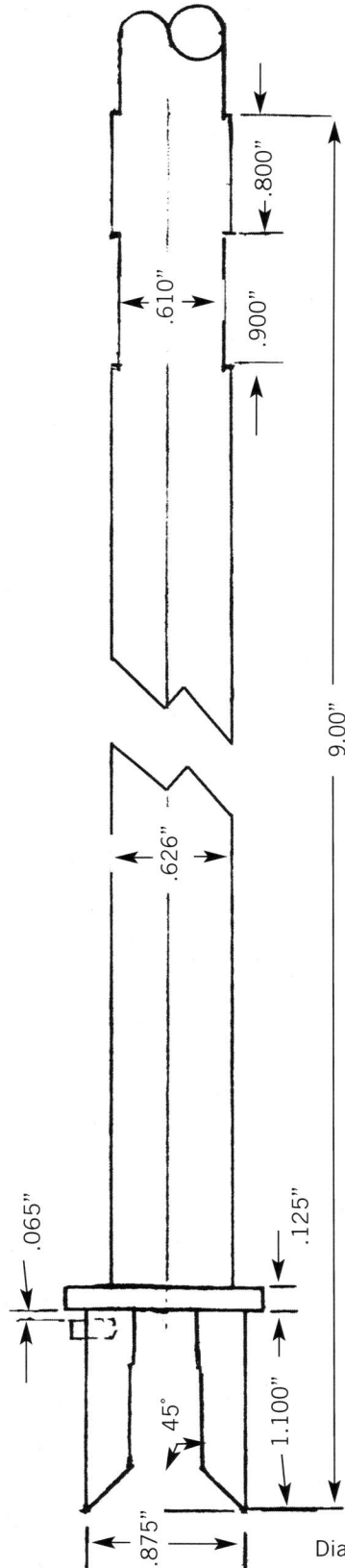

.875"

.600"

7.00" MIN.

RIFLE BARREL

.800"

.610"

.900"

9.00"

.626"

.065"

.125"

45°

1.100"

.875"

BARRELS

Diagram #7

a reamer pilot of bore diameter or slightly less. Of course, most 9mm and .45 ACP cartridges are used in full and semiautomatic arms, but there are also revolvers chambered for these calibers. Just to be on the safe side, go ahead and specify that the reamers are for rifle barrels.

It should be noted that the higher-priced reamers will usually come with an integral throat reamer, allowing you to perform the entire chambering operation with a single reamer. Many times the cheaper ones will require the use of a separate "throating" reamer to cut this portion, which is actually a bullet seat. The higher-priced reamers such as those made by Clymer Manufacturing Co. will usually prove to be the cheapest in the long run, or at least the most convenient.

Construction of the barrel is a fairly simple process. The barrel blank is cut to the desired length and the ends are squared in the lathe. Don't be surprised if, once the barrel blank has been cut in two, the bore is not concentric with the outside diameter. This is a fairly common occurrence, especially with cheaper barrel blanks. If such is the case, the barrel should be mounted between centers and the entire length turned round. The breech end is then turned to a diameter of .875 inch for a length of 1.125 inches. Just ahead of this cylindrical section, which fits inside the upper receiver, a flange .125 inch wide and 1 inch in diameter is formed. The remainder should be turned to a diameter of .600 to .625 inch if used in the 9mm pistol version. The .45-caliber pistol version should be .650 inch or slightly larger in diameter.

The rifle barrel is made in the same fashion, with the same dimensions at the breech end. The portion directly forward of the retaining flange can be slightly larger than the pistol version for a length of 6 inches if desired. The remainder, or the portion that extends past the fore-end, can be turned as small as .550 inch in diameter for the 9mm and should be no larger than .615 inch. This should be the minimum diameter for the .45 barrel. Just forward of the fore-end's front face, two bands should be turned to a diameter of .626 inch. These should be 1/2 inch in length with a relieved section (.610 to .615 inch diameter) .900 inch in length

between them. This will allow a military surplus M16 front sight to fit snugly over the two bands while sliding freely over the barrel until almost in place. This is done primarily to avoid marring the finish when assembling the finished gun.

A 45-degree "approach cone" is formed in the breech end of the barrel to aid in feeding. With this type of feeding system, which is similar to that used in the 1903 Springfield, 1917 Enfield, M54 and M70 Winchesters, as well as several others, the bullet is positively guided into the chamber as it moves forward. This tends to eliminate the "stovepiping" and hangups on the end of the barrel that are fairly common with some other systems.

The muzzle should be crowned with a rounded outer edge and a convex curve on the inside. This will leave a sharp edge where the bore exits the barrel instead of the rounded curve often seen. A lathe cutting tool is ground to form this contour. It can be brought to a high polish with progressively finer grits of abrasive cloth and paper. This type of crown is fully as accurate as the so-called "target" type flat crown with a second flat counterbore inside, which, although it has been used for at least a hundred years, is "discovered" at frequent intervals by some of the newer gunsmiths.

Proper depth of the chamber is determined by measuring from the front face of the receiver to the bolt face, making sure the bolt is fully forward while this measurement is taken. Another measurement is taken from the breech end of the barrel to the retaining flange. This measurement will be slightly longer than the first, so the smaller (first) number is subtracted from the larger. The result will be the depth of the cartridge head below the end of the barrel.

The chamber is cut by feeding the reamer into the end of the barrel that is chucked in the lathe and turning at the slowest speed available. Pressure from the tail stock ram is used to push the reamer into the bore. Do not attempt to hold the reamer with the tail stock chuck. It must be kept from turning by using a hand-held tap wrench, a clamp, a small wrench, or some similar arrangement that can be released and allowed to turn with the barrel in the event the reamer

Approach cone is cut in breech end.

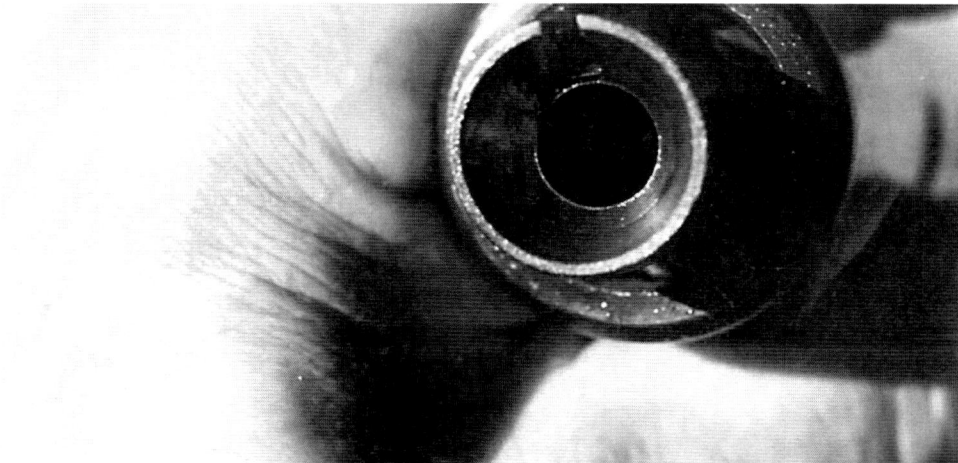

Breech end of barrel, showing approach cone.

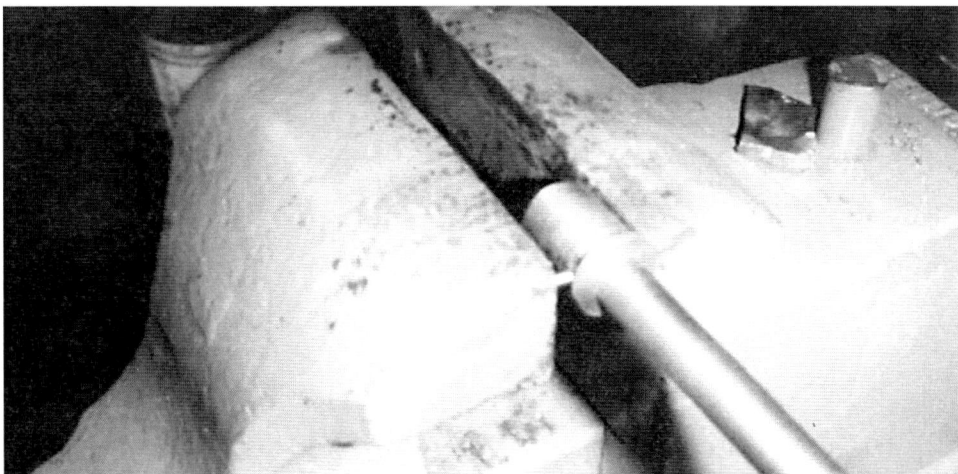

Indexing pin is pressed in place using vise jaws.

should seize. The reamer should be kept well lubricated and withdrawn and cleaned frequently.

Supporting the drive end of the reamer on a tail stock center should only be done when the bore is absolutely concentric, without runout, and the tail stock is absolutely in line and centered with the bore. Otherwise, a flat-faced center with a small dimple in the middle should be used to push the reamer.

Another method is to clamp the barrel between wood blocks in a vise and turn the reamer by hand using a suitable tap wrench or reamer drive. If this method is used, care must be taken to hold the reamer straight and in line with the bore, with no sideways pressure exerted in any direction.

A small hole is drilled, as shown in Diagram #7, using a No. 31 drill, and after a slight taper is ground on one end, a locating pin made from 1/8-inch drill rod is pressed into it. This causes the barrel to be replaced in the same position after removal.

The extractor slot is located and cut as described in the chapter on fitting and assembly.

BARREL SHROUD, STOCK, AND GRIP

If the commercial lower receiver assembly is used, we will only need to concern ourselves with the barrel shroud, as used on the pistol version, or the fore-end, as used on the rifle. Both are identical except for overall length and the fact that a cap is welded in place in the front end of the rifle fore-end.

Each is begun by turning a barrel retaining nut to the shape and dimensions shown in Diagram #9. It is threaded on the inside to screw on the front end of the receiver. It has a shoulder inside that bears against the barrel flange when tightened, securing the barrel in place. This nut should be made from a better grade of steel such as 4140 or automobile axle material. The threads may stretch and wear rapidly if low carbon steel such as 1018 is used.

The cylindrical portion can be made from almost any thin-walled tubing of the correct outside diameter. Since there is no strength requirement here, even muffler pipe can be used, provided the unsightly seam that is usually present is acceptable. Discarded automobile shock absorbers are a good source for material such as this, provided the right size can be found. Actually, the outside diameter can be adjusted up or down to accommodate the available material. In fact, when used with the pistol version, a barrel shroud slightly smaller than the receiver diameter would probably look better than the one illustrated in Diagram #8.

Both versions should be a snug fit over the outside of the nut and are welded or silver-soldered in place. The rifle version should have an end cap, which is turned to a snug fit inside the tubing and then welded or silver-soldered in place at the forward end. It must also have a hole bored through the center, slightly larger than the barrel diameter.

The ventilating holes in the shroud body can be spaced to suit your taste. The prototype had four rows of 1/2-inch holes spaced 1.200 inches apart. These can be accurately and easily spaced and drilled in the milling machine. If the holes are started with a center drill and finished with a radius-nosed 1/2-inch end mill, smoother holes will result than if the work is done with a twist drill.

Commercial pistol grips are available from a number of sources, some with the original military configuration and others with numerous modifications and refinements. These are available at such low prices that it would seem foolish to manufacture one.

Should it become necessary, however, it is a fairly simple matter to build one. A block of whatever type of hardwood that suits your fancy is obtained. Since it only needs to be 1 1/4 inches thick, 2 1/4 inches wide, and 5 inches long, such a scrap can usually be found at a cabinet or custom furniture shop. Custom gun stock makers and knife makers are also sources for these.

The outline is drawn on the side of the blank

FORE-END

RIFLE VERSION

6.500"

1.500"

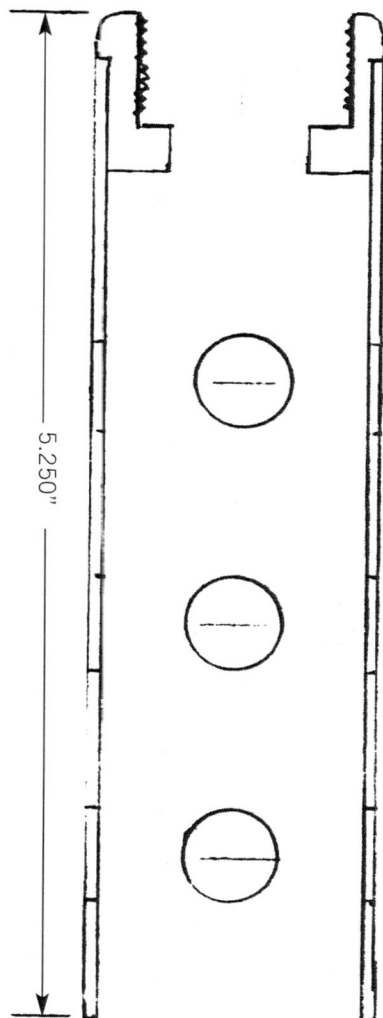

PISTOL VERSION

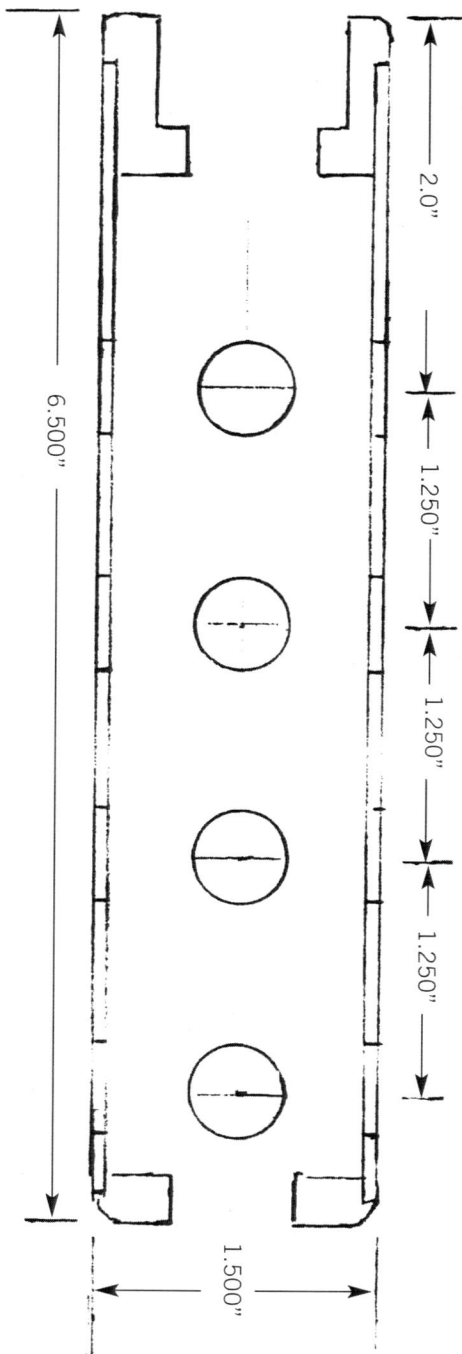

5.250"

2.0"

1.250"

1.250"

1.250"

Diagram #8

32

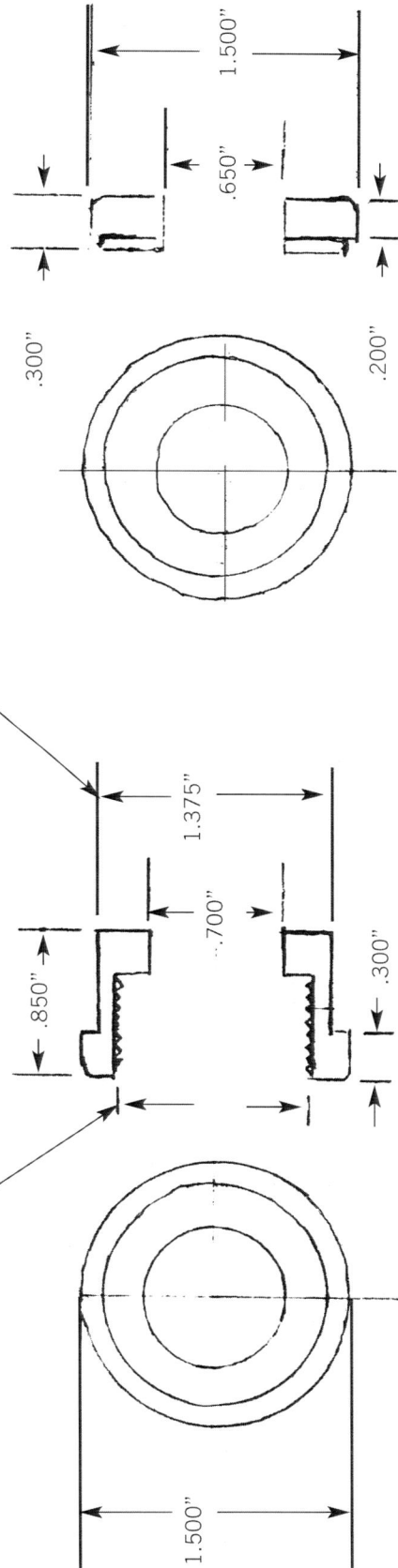

1.500"

.650"

.300"

.200"

FRONT PLUG

TURN TO A SNUG
FIT INSIDE TUBING

1.375"

.700"

.850"

.300"

BORE 1.080" THREAD
1.125" x 24

BARREL NUT

1.500"

FORE-END COMPONENTS

Diagram #9

33

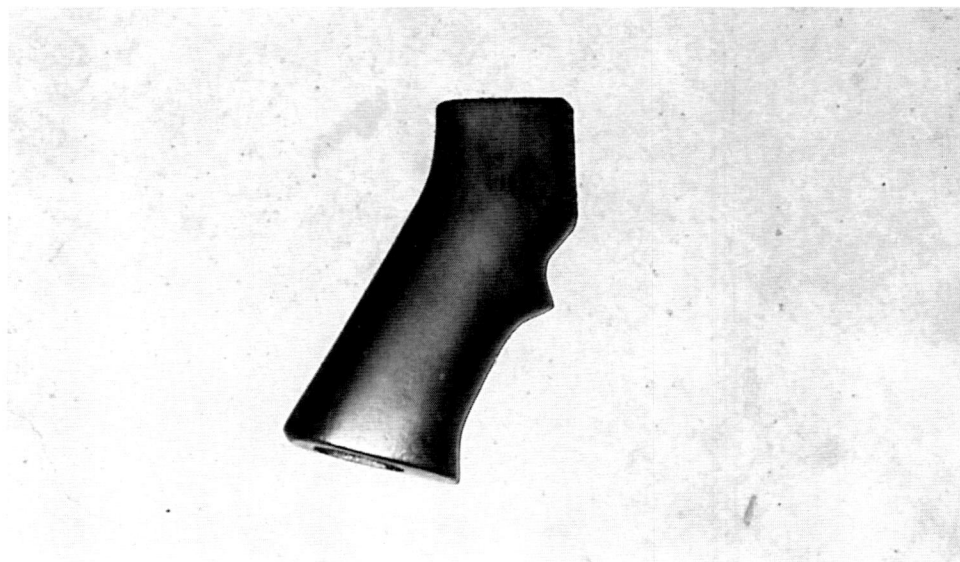

Grip was made of walnut, painted black simply because I didn't have a plastic military-surplus grip on hand.

using the pattern shown in Diagram #10, or whatever profile suits you, and cut to shape. It is then clamped in the milling machine and the top side is shaped to mate with the receiver. The top and front side where it fits against the receiver are milled flat and square. This is followed by canting the blank at the required angle and cutting the slot. The hole for the mounting bolt should be drilled while this angle is set. The hole's location can be determined by measuring from the center of the bolt hole in the receiver to the flat part of the receiver that the grip adjoins and transferring this measurement to the grip blank. The grip is then reversed and either a counterbore to clear the head of the mounting bolt hole or a cavity similar to the one found in the commercial grip is cut in the lower end. This should be parallel to the mounting bolt hole, and it can be done with a 5/8-inch end mill.

The outside contour is formed using the sanding wheel to rough-shape it and finishing with rasp files and sandpaper in progressively finer grits (starting with 50 or 60 grit and finishing up with 400 grit).

The finish used can be any kind or color that strikes your fancy, from clear gun stock finish to camouflage paint. The grip shown in the photographs was made from a walnut block and

given several coats of automobile primer. This was followed by several coats of flat black enamel in an attempt to match the color of the butt stock. My only reason for building it in the first place was that I wanted it on a certain day and none were available locally. A bit of planning and ordering ahead would have saved me this extra work, but I suppose I need the experience.

The butt stock, as available on the surplus parts market, is another bargain. Mounting it in place presents no problem. If the action spring and buffer housing are on hand, you simply screw it into the lower receiver and slip the butt stock over it. It is held in place by a screw that installs through the butt plate.

When the short, self-contained bolt assembly is used, this part is not necessary. A plug is turned from aluminum (if available—to save weight) to the dimensions shown in Diagram #11 and threaded to screw into the lower receiver. It is drilled and tapped in the center for a 1/4 x 28 thread. A draw bolt, which extends to the rear of the stock, is cut from 1/4-inch drill rod and threaded with the same 1/4 x 28 thread to screw into the receiver plug. A 3/8-inch-diameter sleeve, 1 1/2 inches long, is drilled to approximately half depth with a 1/4-inch drill, slipped over the smooth end of the draw bolt, and silver-soldered

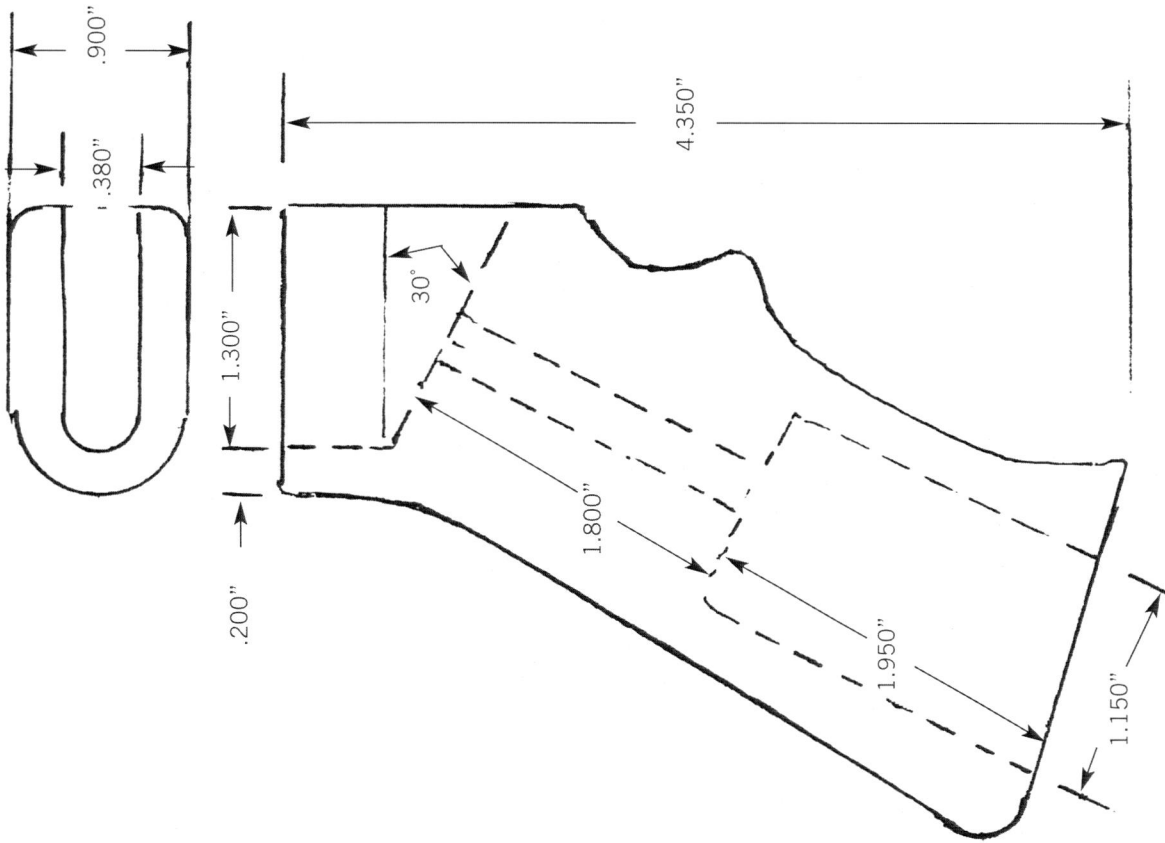

.900"

.380"

4.350"

30°

1.300"

.200"

1.800"

1.950"

1.150"

SHOP-MADE GRIP

Diagram #10

35

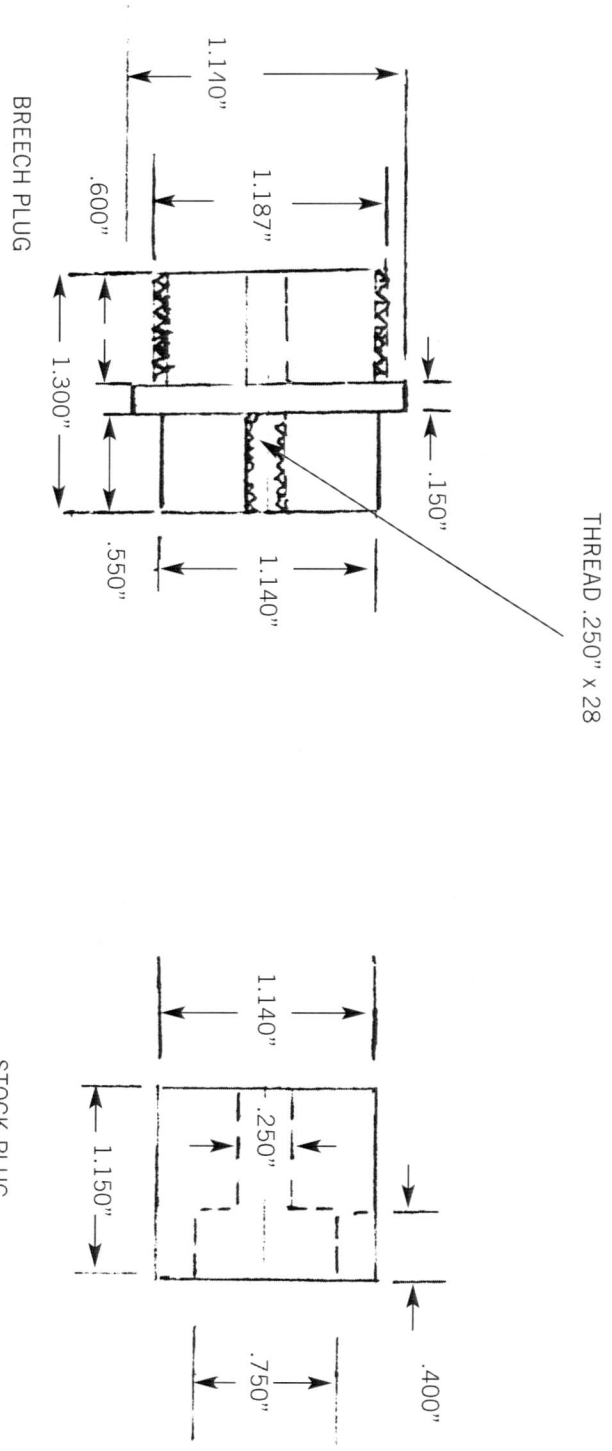

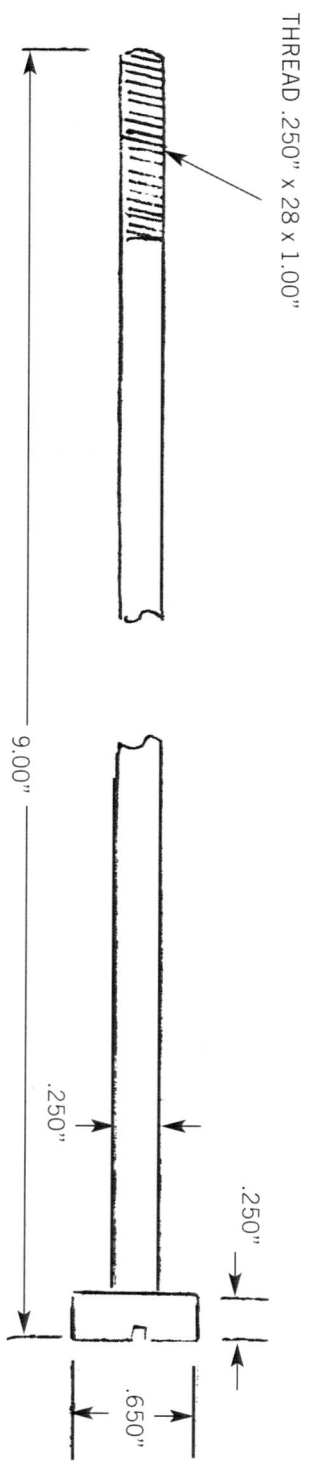

STOCK BOLT PARTS REQUIRED TO MOUNT SURPLUS M16/AR-15 BUTT STOCK

BREECH PLUG

1.110"

1.187"

.600"

1.300"

.550"

1.140"

.150"

THREAD .250" x 28

THREAD .250" x 28 x 1.00"

9.00"

.250"

.250"

.650"

STOCK PLUG

1.140"

1.150"

.250"

.750"

.400"

Diagram #11

36

BORE .217" THREAD .250" x 28

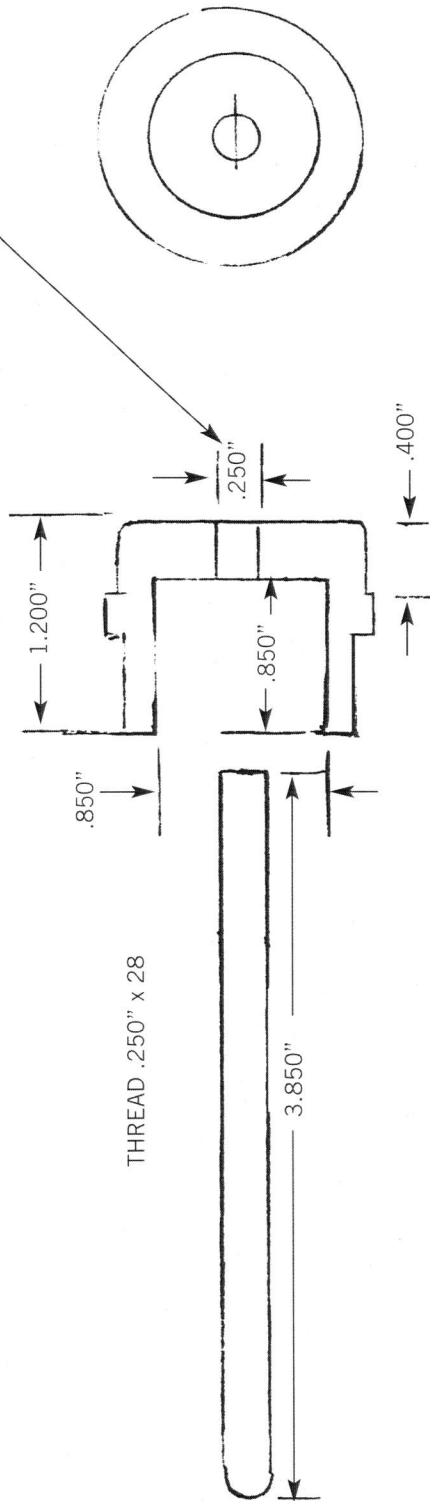

.250"

.400"

1.200"

.850"

.850"

THREAD .250" x 28

3.850"

DELETE SPRING GUIDE WHEN
USED WITH CLOSED BOLT

1.375"

1.300"

.200"

.600"

THREAD 1.187" x 16

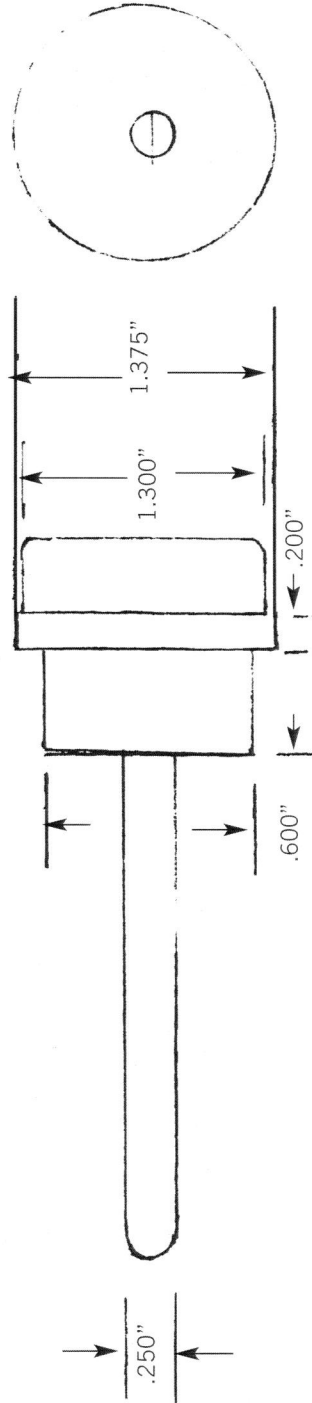

.250"

REAR RECEIVER CAP FOR OPEN-BOLT PISTOL VERSION

Diagram #12

37

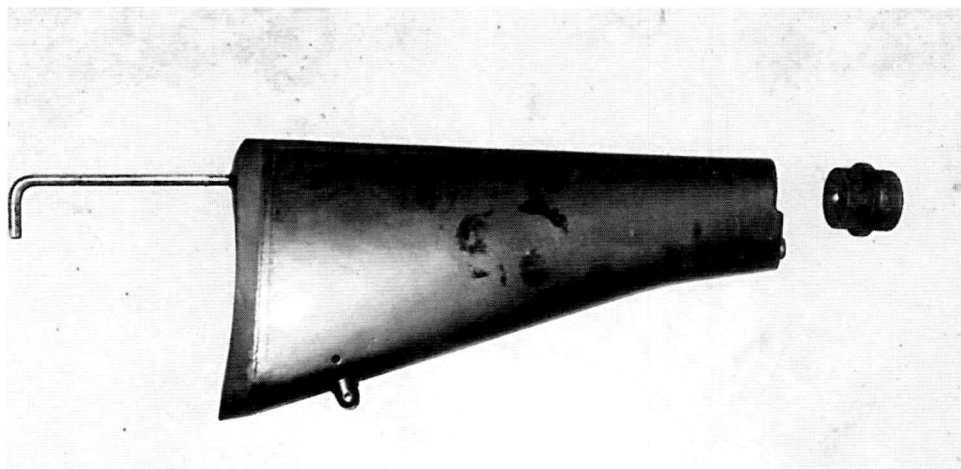

Surplus M16 butt stock is mounted using through bolt and breech plug adaptor. Recoil pad is added for extra length.

Breech plug screws into lower receiver. Through-bolt screws into rear end of plug.

in place. The remainder is drilled and tapped for a 10 x 32 screw. This arrangement allows the butt stock to be positioned in place and a short 10 x 32 screw installed through the butt plate, which, when tightened, holds the butt stock in place.

For a full-grown man, it is desirable that the butt stock be somewhat longer than the length provided by the standard military M16 butt stock.

For some reason, our military has always—even from flintlock musket times—used rifles with a short enough length of pull to accommodate the very smallest shooter, and everyone else is expected to adapt to it. The butt plate portion can be removed by sawing and squared with the sanding wheel, after which a recoil pad is epoxied in place. This will lengthen the pull by 1/2 to 1

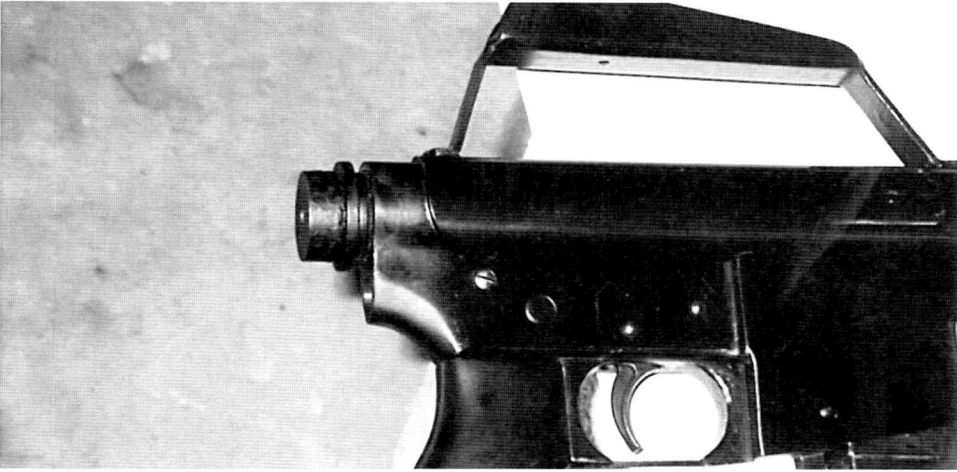

Breech plug partially screwed in place.

Through-bolt is secured using allen wrench through recoil pad.

inch, depending on the thickness of the pad. If this is done, another close-fitting aluminum spacer is epoxied in place in the rear end of the stock. It should also be pinned in place with a 1/8-inch steel cross pin, installed through a hole drilled through the plug and both stock walls. This should be drilled offset from the center hole so as to not interfere with the draw bolt. The outside end of this plug should be counterbored to accept a bolt head, which is welded or silver-soldered to the end of the stock bolt, replacing the threaded sleeve. This should be a bolt head that accepts an allen wrench. If the upper mounting screw hole in the recoil pad is enlarged enough to clear the allen wrench, the butt stock can be installed or removed without the bolt head showing.

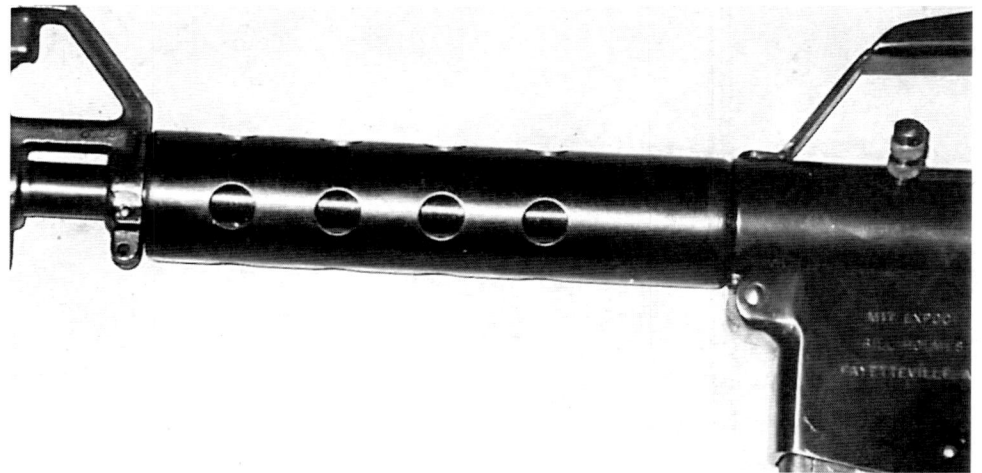

Finished fore-end installed on completed gun.

If the time ever comes when the military-type stocks are no longer available, it will be simple enough to make a butt stock from hardwood, just as we did the grip. This would require a draw bolt hole extending from the front face of the stock, partway through to the rear, with the remainder enlarged to clear the bolt head. The threaded plug in the receiver would be counterbored at the rear to accept a round tenon, machined or carved on the front face of the stock. A short metal pin, which fits into the recess in the receiver to keep the stock from turning, would be threaded into the stock face just below the tenon. Your choice of butt plate or recoil pad is fitted to the butt end and the assembly shaped and finished in the same fashion as the grip.

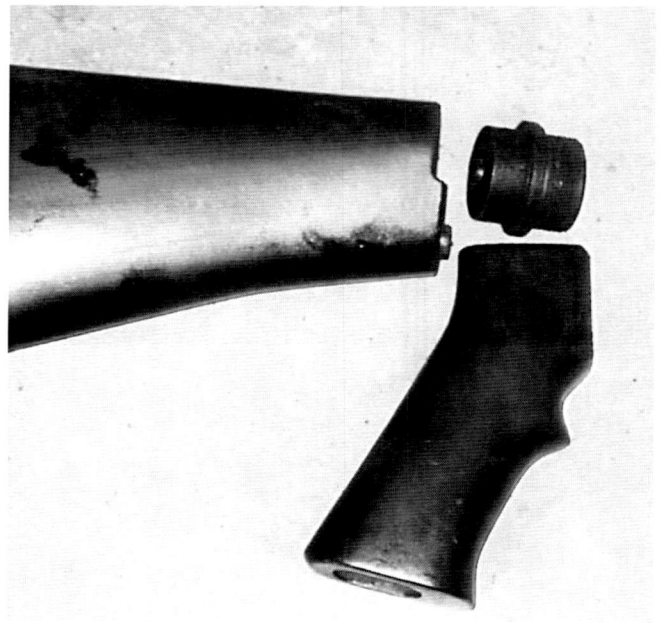

Grip, butt stock, and adaptor.

SIGHTS

Sights, as used on the pistol version, are practically identical to those used on my other pistol designs, differing only in that the radius at the base is slightly larger. At the risk of being considered repetitious, I will include directions on how to make such sights here for those who don't have my other books.

Experience has shown me that elaborate adjustable sights are not necessary on the pistol version of this gun. A simple blade front sight and a fixed, square-notched rear, when aligned and cut to the proper heights, are completely adequate for a gun of this type.

Bases, complete with protective ears, can easily be formed from 16-gauge sheet metal using a vise, form blocks, and a heavy hammer.

The form block, which can be used to form both front and rear bases, is made by cutting a radius to match the contour of the receiver on the lower side of a steel block. Since the receiver is 1 1/2 inches in diameter, the radius cut should match this plus the thickness of the sheet metal used. The block should be .625 inch wide by .750 inch high and at least 1 inch long. This will form the inside of the sight bases. A short length of 1 1/2-inch-diameter round stock is used to form the convex bottom side, which fits against the receiver. Two 1/8-inch-diameter holes, .625 inch

Pistol sight blanks shown with form die.

Blank is placed on form die.

PISTOL SIGHTS

FRONT SIGHT

.125" X .750" SLOT

.700"

.400"

FORM FROM 14 ga. SHEET METAL BLADES FROM .125"

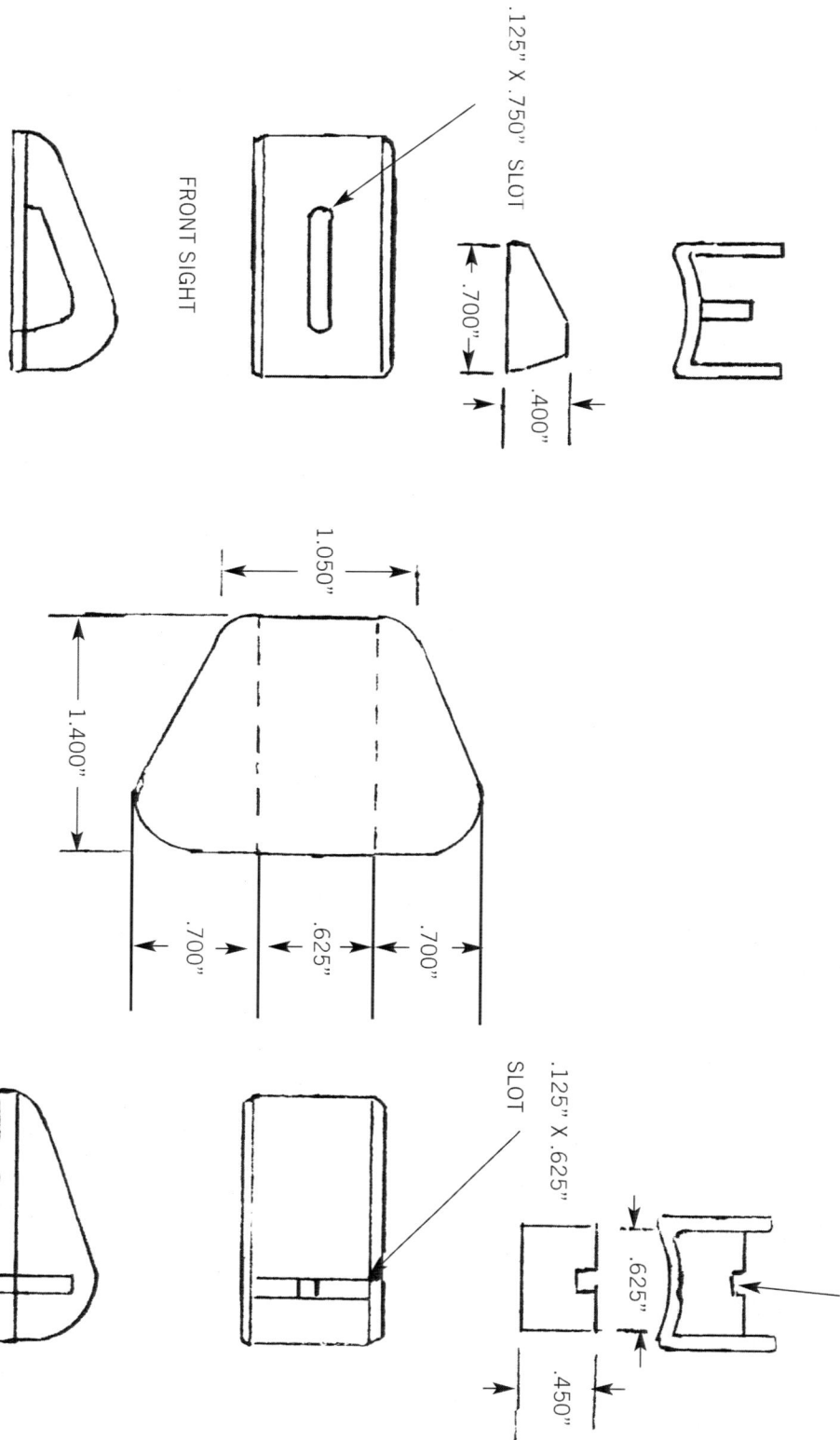

1.050"

1.400"

.700"

.625"

.700"

SLOT

.125" X .625"

.625"

.450"

Diagram #13

42

Formed to shape in vise.

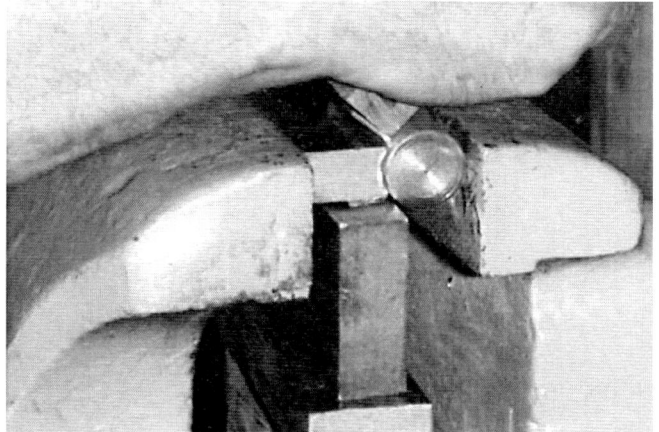

Sides are folded over with hammer.

Formed front sight base with blade.

Formed rear sight base.

Rear sight base with sight blank.

apart, should be drilled on center, completely through the form block. These should continue partway through the lower, round form block. Locating pins installed in these holes keep the assembly aligned while in use.

Blanks are cut, as shown in Diagram #13, with holes drilled to match the locating pin holes. The bases will form more easily if left in a rectangular shape until formed and the upright ears cut to shape after forming. With the locating pins in place, the blank is positioned between both form blocks and the assembly clamped, with one side down, in the vise. When the vise is tightened, pressure from the vise jaws will form the radiused bottom portion.

Sights mounted in place.

The part of the blank extending above the form blocks is bent, or folded, flat against the side of the form block using a block and heavy hammer. At this point the assembly is reversed, or turned over, in the vise and the process repeated. It is helpful to place a spacer, or a series of blocks (sometimes called "blocking up") between the throat of the vise and the bottom of the part being formed. This will prevent both the work and the form blocks from being driven deeper in the vise when forming.

A slot is cut crosswise in one base to receive the rear sight cross piece and lengthwise down the center of the other for the front sight blade. These can be cut with a 1/8-inch end mill, or, if necessary, with a high-speed hand grinder using a cut-off blade.

The blades are fluxed and silver-soldered in place in the bases. Both assemblies are then clamped in place on the receiver and silver-soldered. Both sights can be kept in alignment during mounting by placing a close-fitting (5/8-

inch-wide) piece of square stock, long enough to reach across both sights, inside both bases and clamping it in place before mounting.

For those who absolutely must have adjustable sights, the rear sight cross piece can be omitted and the base drilled and tapped for a Williams "Guide" rear sight, which is adjustable for both windage and elevation. A Marble #20 rear sight, which is almost identical to the aluminum Williams sight except that it is made of steel, can also be used. Either of these will serve the purpose. If you simply must have one that you made yourself, my book entitled *Home Workshop Weapons for Defense and Resistance: Vol. I, The Submachine Gun* contains a description of one that is adaptable.

The rifle version requires the combination of a rear sight base and a carrying handle that elevates the rear sight to the same height as the commercial gun.

The base is made by cutting a blank to the shape and dimensions shown in the drawing from

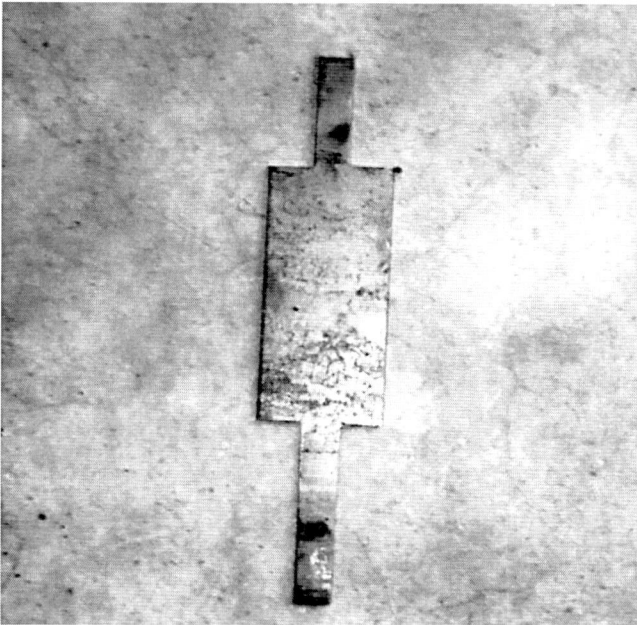

Rifle rear sight base is cut from 12 ga. sheet steel.

Placed in vise against form block.

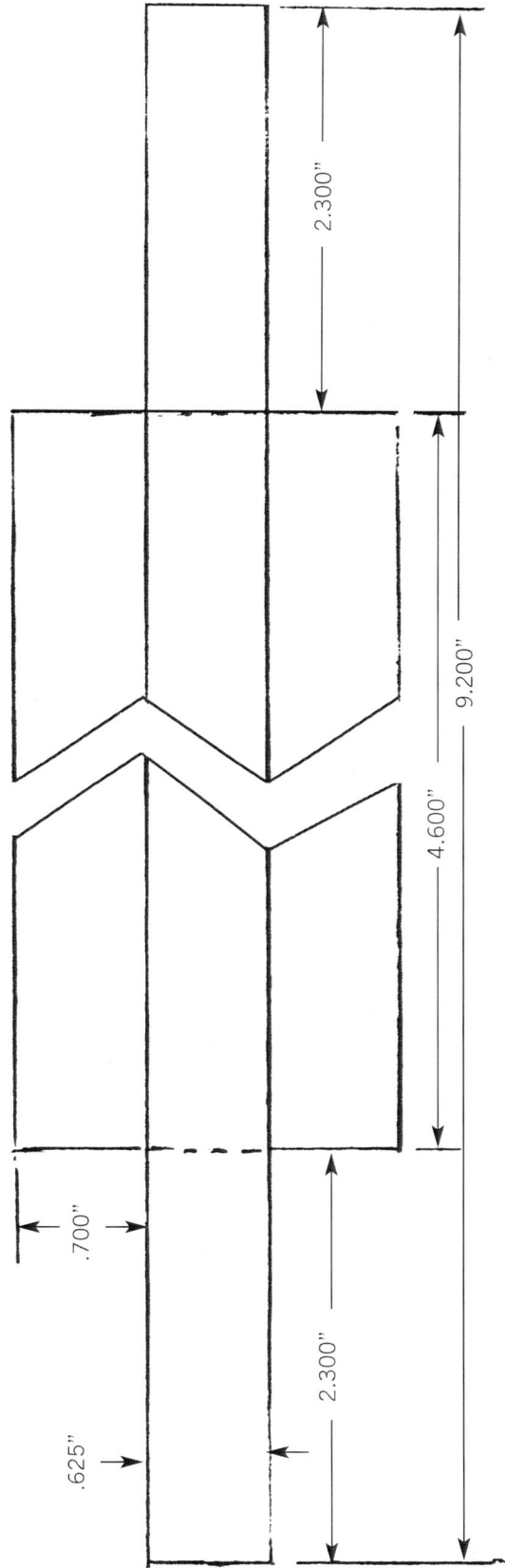

2.300"

9.200"

4.600"

.700"

2.300"

.625"

RIFLE REAR SIGHT PATTERN

Diagram #14

45

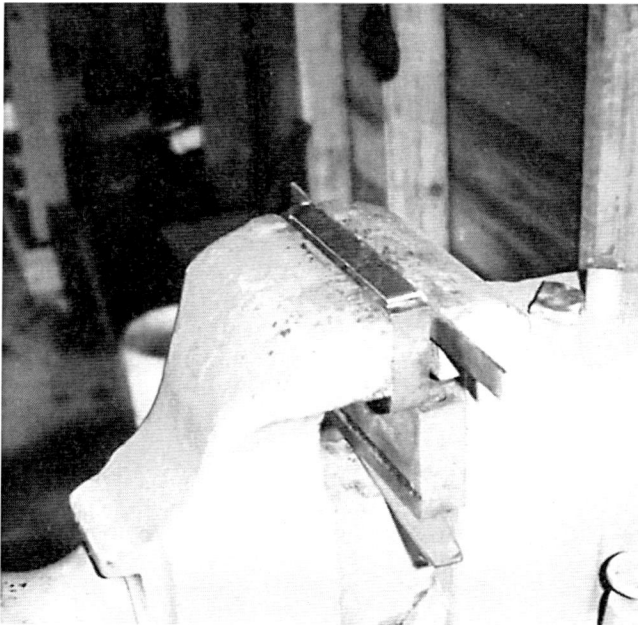

Sides are formed with black and hammer.

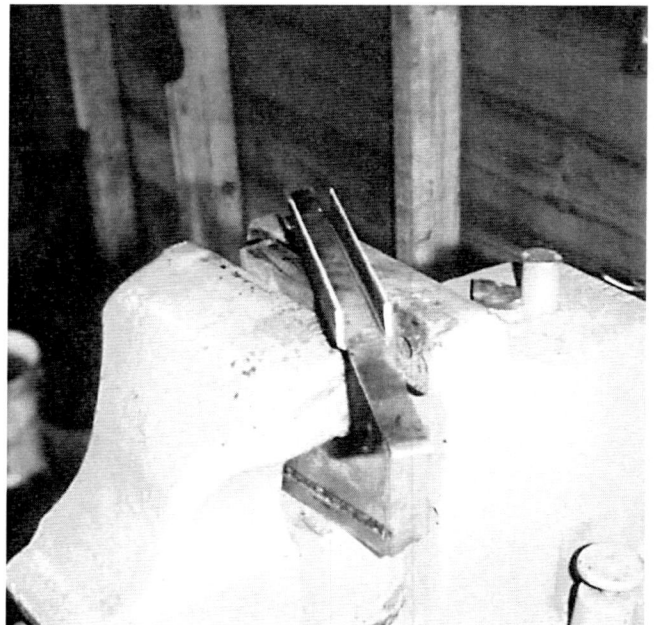

Shaped rear sight.

12-gauge sheet metal. The blank is then clamped in the vise against a form block of 5/8-inch-thick steel bar stock, which should be at least 3/4 inch wide and 5 or more inches long. Here again, this form block should be supported by blocking it up between the bottom of the block and the throat of the vise. When struck with a heavy hammer, work such as this has a tendency to move downward between the vise jaws unless supported

underneath. The portion extending above the fold line is bent flat against the side of the form block using the hammer and a flat piece of bar stock. When formed, the assembly is turned over and the opposite side is formed in the same manner, creating a hollow trough. The sides are then shaped to the profile shown in Diagram #14 or whatever shape appeals to you.

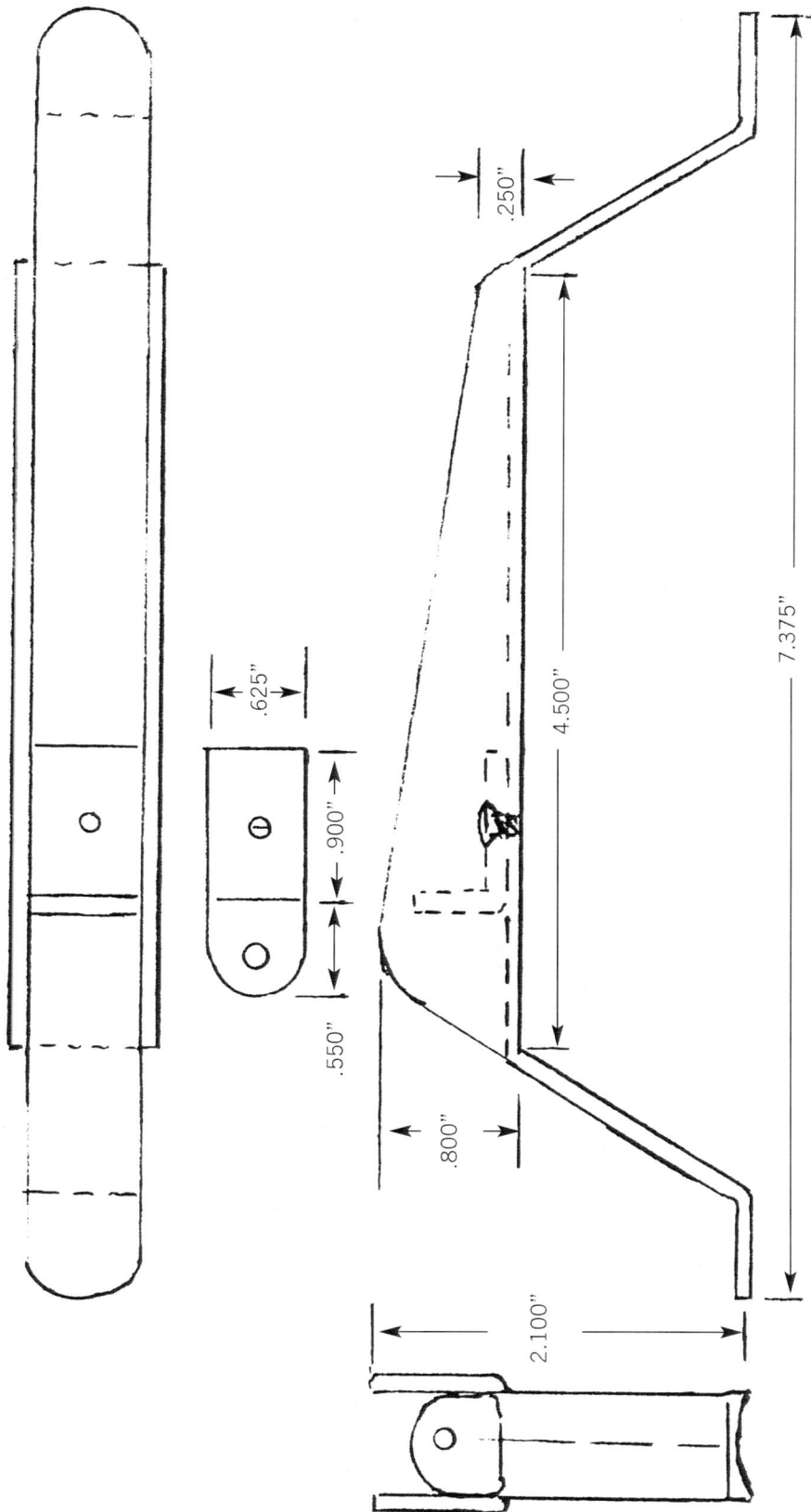

REAR SIGHT/CARRYING HANDLE RIFLE VERSION

.250"

7.375"

4.500"

.625"

.900"

.550"

.800"

2.100"

Diagram #15

Rear sight with legs bent to shape.

Finished rear sight mounted in place.

The legs are formed by bending the narrow flat portion extending from the ends of the trough downward approximately 150 degrees, or 30 degrees from the vertical. A line parallel to the bottom of the trough portion is marked 1.400 inches below the trough. The mounting tabs are bent to a point where they match a flat surface. These should be sharp bends formed by a block and hammer. The resulting tabs should be cut to match the radius of the receiver. This can be done in the milling machine using a large ball cutter, or it can be ground and filed to fit.

A simple fixed rear sight can be made from a strip of 14-gauge sheet metal with a leg bent upward at 90 degrees and drilled for a peep sight hole. The horizontal portion, together with the base, is drilled and tapped for at least one mounting screw. Since this version can be better

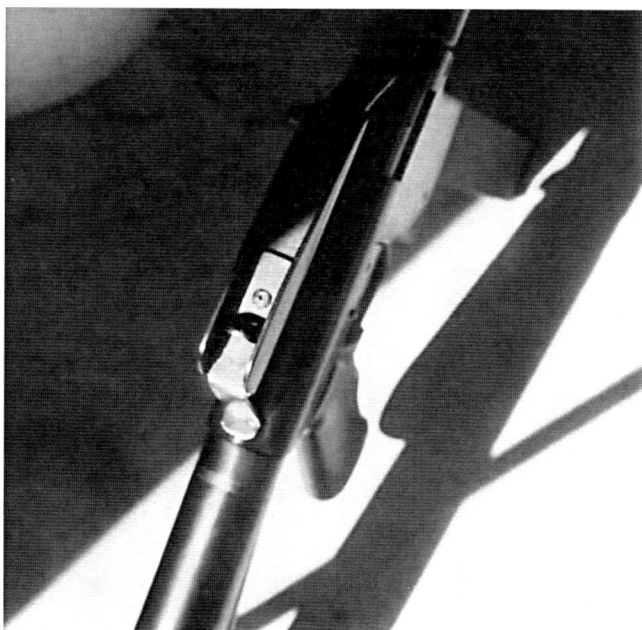

Aperture sight in place.

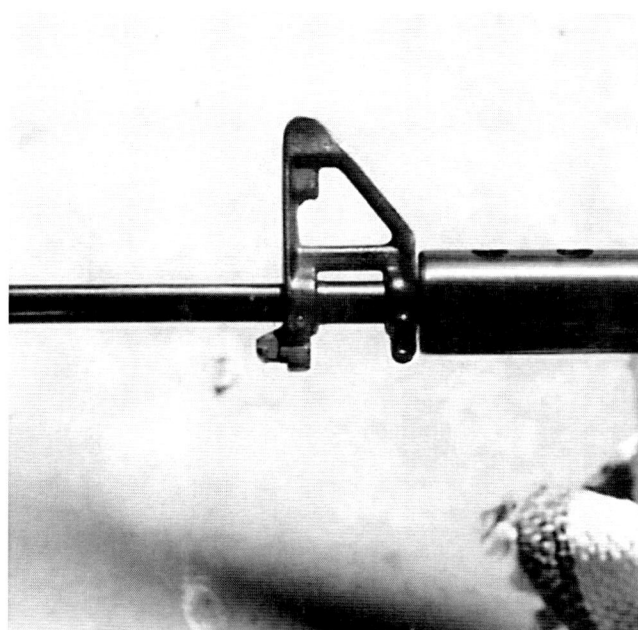

Surplus front sight mounted on barrel.

served with adjustable sights, Williams or Marble sights should be used. Mounting holes for either of these should be drilled and tapped before the base is attached to the receiver.

The underside of the base should be polished to an acceptable level for finishing before mounting. An easy way to locate the base on the receiver in a true vertical position is to clamp the receiver in the milling machine vise. Then, with the mounting tabs fluxed, the base is located in position and held by a sharp-pointed rod chucked in the milling machine quill. The cross feed is used to move the receiver from side to side until the base is aligned vertically using a square or plumb bob for verification. It is then silver-soldered in place.

A military surplus M16 front sight, which is readily available from surplus parts dealers, is easily mounted. This should be a snug fit over the collars left for this purpose on the barrel. Holes for the pins to secure this in place must be continued across the lower side of the barrel using the existing holes in the sight base as guides. These should be cut with a 1/8-inch end mill instead of trying to drill them, since the drill will try to drift, or crawl, to the side where no cutting is done and likely break. These holes should then be reamed slightly using a 9/64-inch taper pin reamer. Pins with a matching taper are pressed tightly in place, securing the sight in position.

An acceptable front sight assembly can be folded from sheet metal and the parts silver-soldered or welded together, but with the low price of the surplus sight, it is hardly worthwhile.

To avoid future problems with federal agents, it might be a good idea to remove the bayonet lug before finishing.

LOWER RECEIVER

As stated earlier, this book was originally intended to encompass only an upper receiver assembly and magazine adapter, which, when installed on a commercial lower receiver assembly, made possible the pistol caliber conversion. But when it became likely that further manufacture of commercial lower receivers would be prohibited when the so-called "Crime Bill" became law, existing lower receivers escalated rapidly in price. The last time I checked, the asking price for one of these had gone from around $60 to more than $400. With this—as well as a probable scarcity—in mind, I decided that a shop-made lower receiver was desirable. The design shown here is intended to conform closely to the commercial configuration and use commercial or surplus parts. Since it is made entirely of steel, it is somewhat heavier than the original alloy job, but it is also quite a bit sturdier.

I have attempted to show here both a receiver made especially for the subcaliber conversion unit and one that will accommodate the original full-size, military-caliber upper receiver. These differ mainly in the length of the magazine opening and the addition of the bolt hold-open device and original magazine latch on the full-size job. The magazine is made just long enough to accept the pistol-caliber magazine, and the magazine latch is moved to the lower side and just behind the opening in the same position as with the magazine adapter used with the commercial receiver.

I also used headless screws instead of push pins to hold both receivers together. This not only eliminates the small springs and detents used in the original, but it is more dependable. While disassembly does require a screwdriver and a couple of minutes of time, it is unlikely that the gun will be rendered dysfunctional due to the push pins being lost, as has happened in the past with the originals.

Construction is begun by cutting the two sheet metal parts from 12-gauge sheet metal to the dimensions shown in the diagrams. Note that two sets of patterns are shown in this chapter. The one is intended for use with the pistol-caliber receiver only and is somewhat simpler to construct than the other, which is intended for use in the same manner as the full-length-magazine original.

If the .223 version is used, an offset slot must be formed to clear the raised magazine catch located on the left side of the magazine. This is done by milling a slot .065 inch deep and .710 inch wide in a piece of heavy steel plate. This forms the female portion of a form die. With the sheet metal panel located in position over the slot, a .500-inch-wide piece of bar stock, used here as a male die, is positioned on the opposite

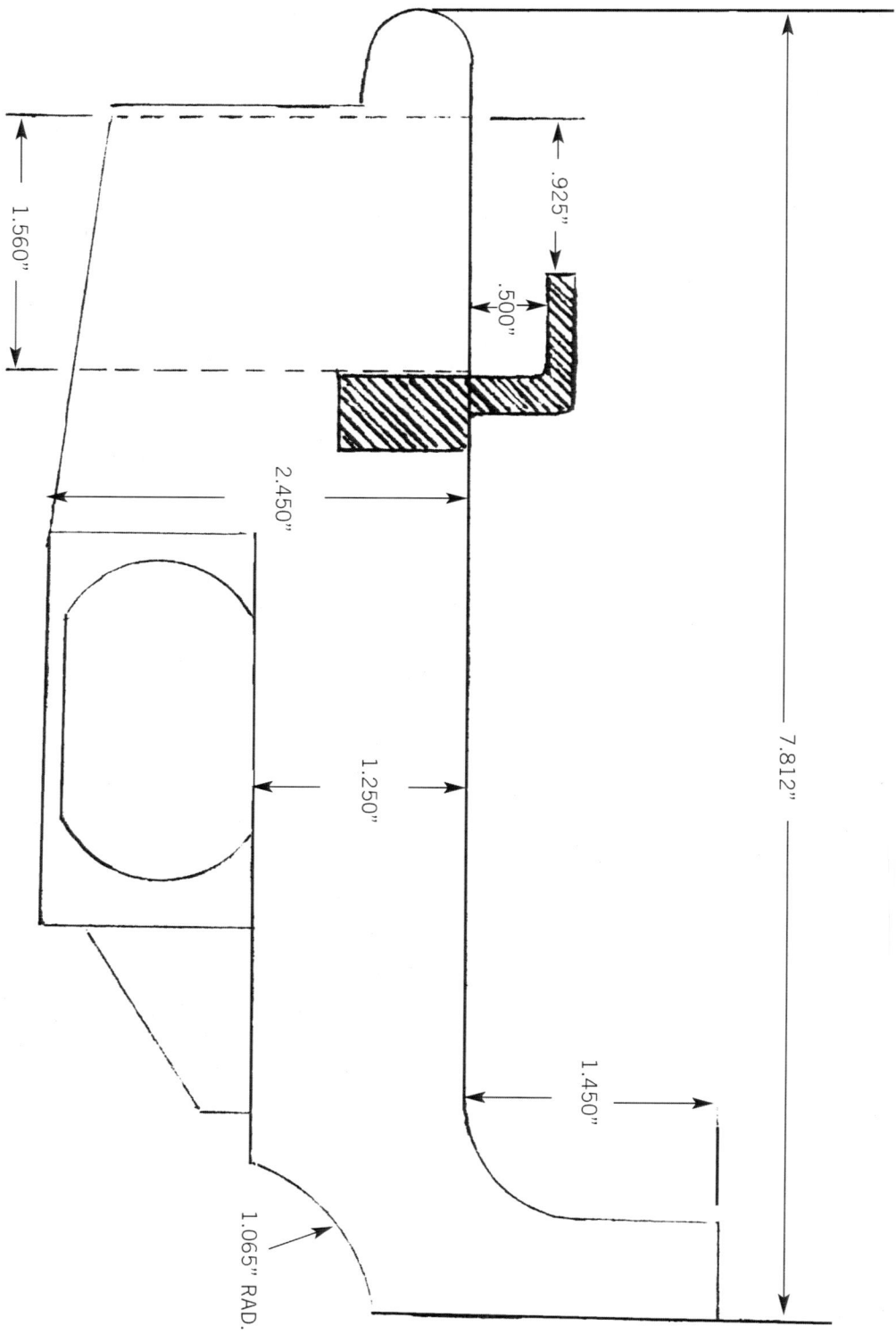

SHOP-MADE LOWER RECEIVER SHOWING EJECTOR LOCATION

1.560"

.925"

.500"

2.450"

1.250"

7.812"

1.450"

1.065" RAD.

Diagram #16

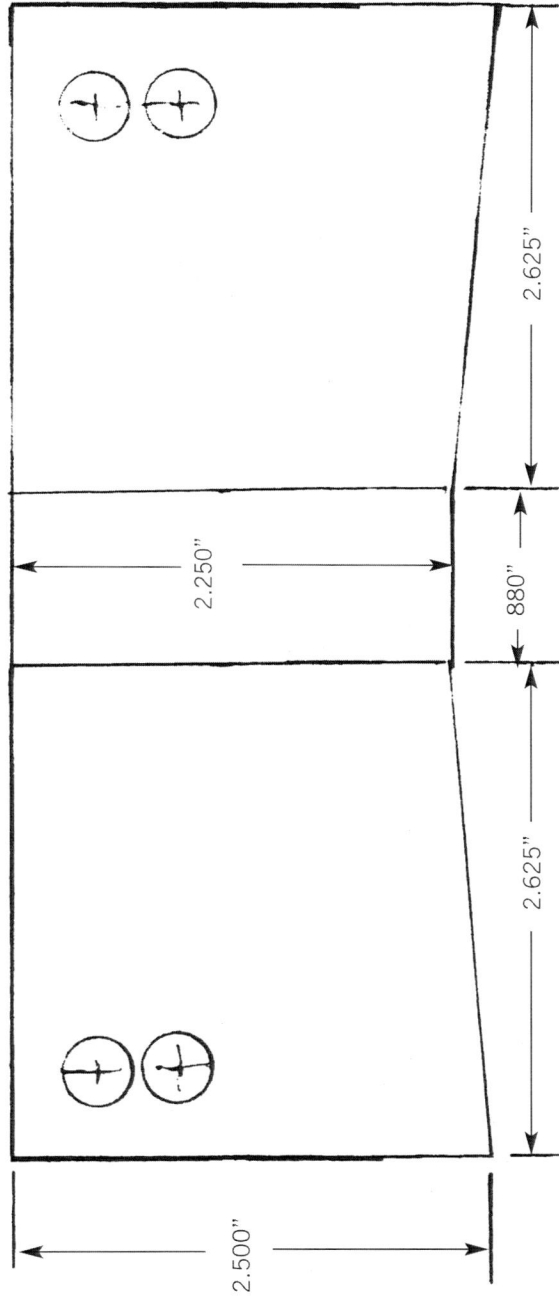

3/8" HOLES TO BE WELDED FLUSH DURING ASSEMBLY

2.250"

2.625"

880"

2.625"

2.500"

FRONT LOWER RECEIVER PATTERN

Diagram #17

REAR LOWER RECEIVER PATTERN

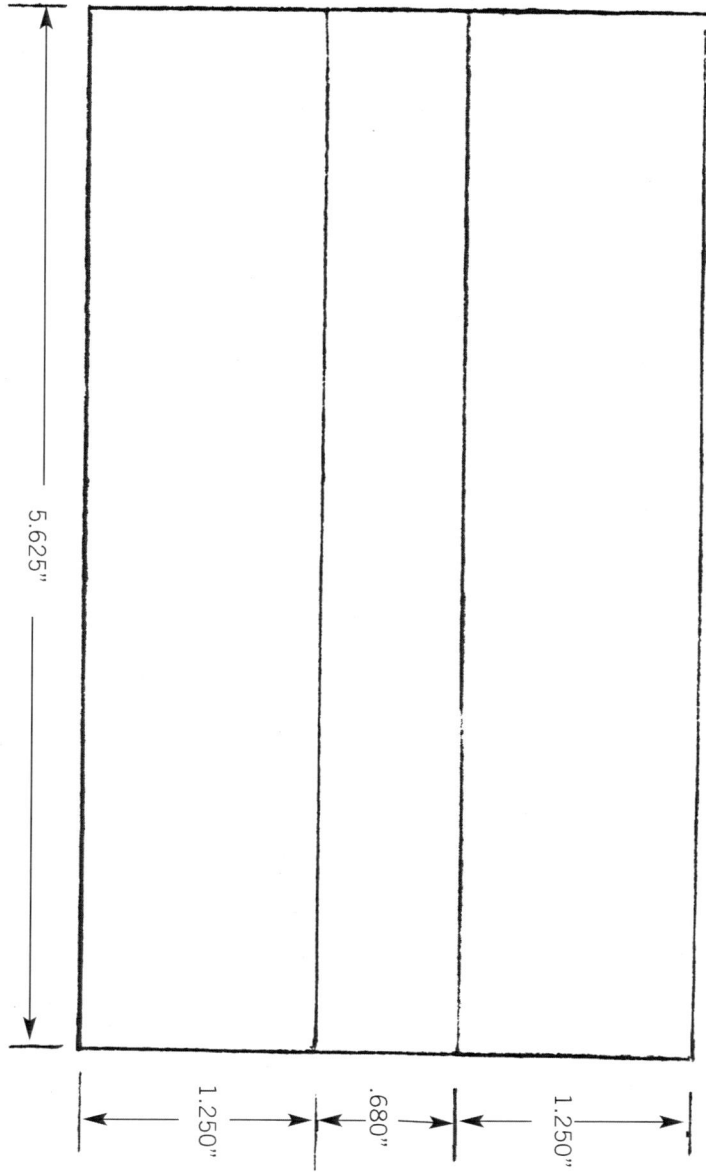

5.625"

1.250"

.680"

1.250"

Diagram #18

Sheet metal parts are cut to size and shape.

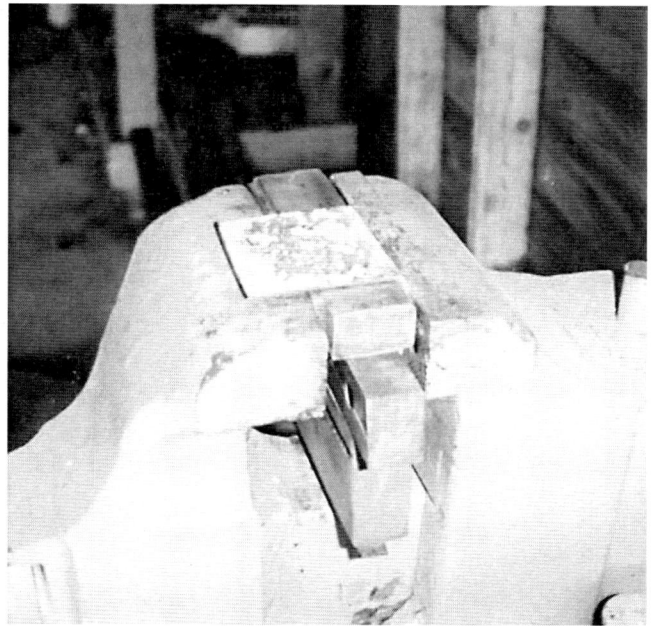
One side folded around form block.

Part is reversed in vise and the opposite side folded.

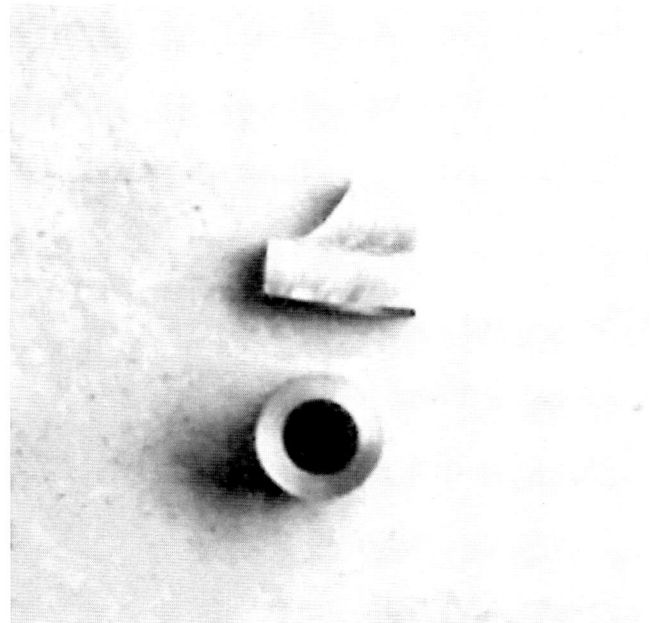
Parts of rear receiver filler and stock mounting bracket.

side of the sheet metal and pressed, squeezed, or hammered until the slot is formed. The photographs above should clarify this. While the required slot probably could be milled into the side of the magazine well, eliminating the forming die process, the remaining metal thickness would only be some .040 inch. The formed slot will retain its original thickness of .100 inch plus, which will be considerably stiffer and stronger, making the extra work worthwhile.

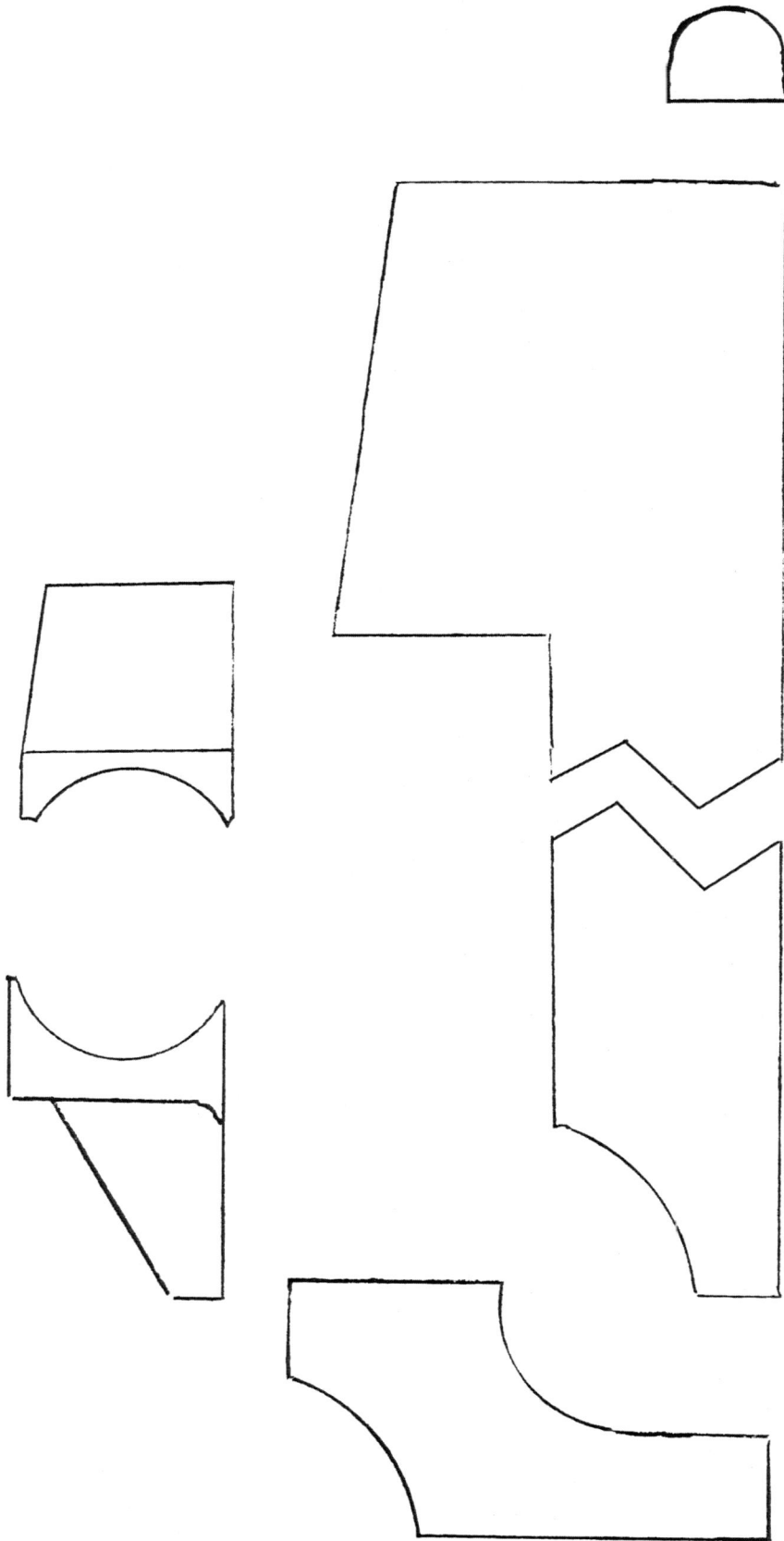

Diagram #19

56

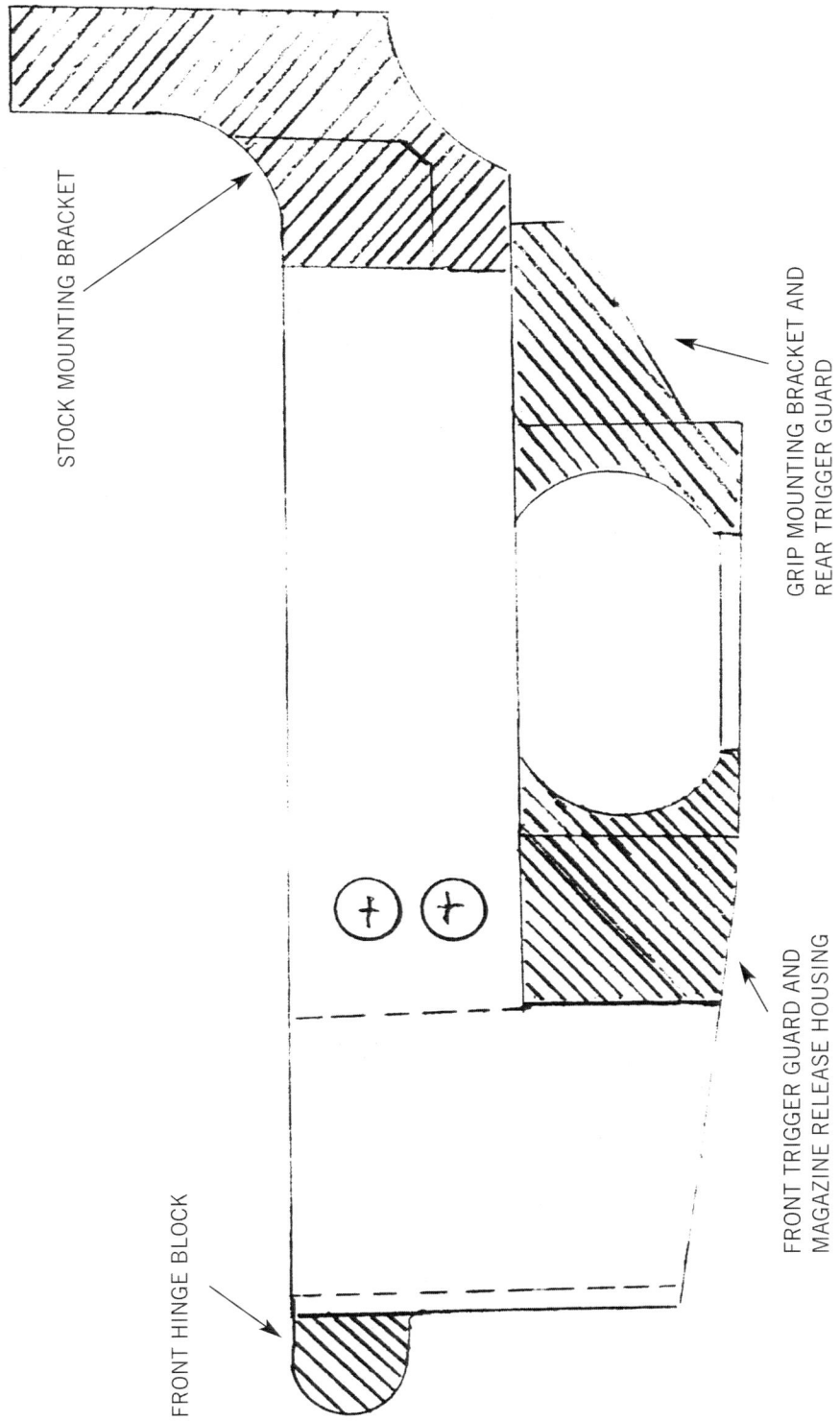

STOCK MOUNTING BRACKET

GRIP MOUNTING BRACKET AND
REAR TRIGGER GUARD

FRONT TRIGGER GUARD AND
MAGAZINE RELEASE HOUSING

FRONT HINGE BLOCK

FRONT LOWER RECEIVER PATTERN

Diagram #20

Components clamped together for welding.

Welded into single unit.

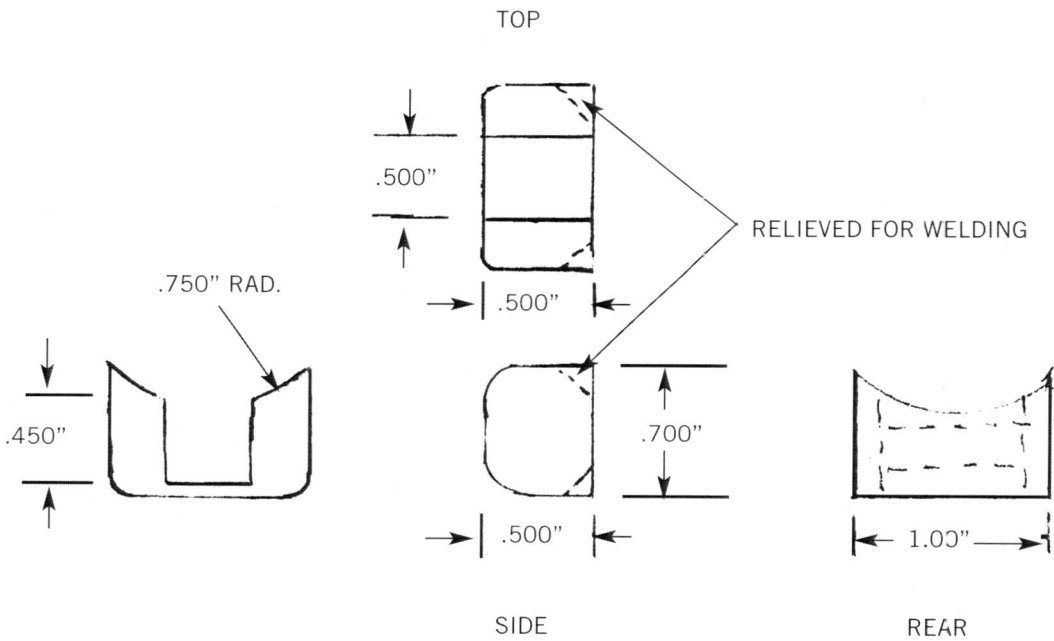

TOP

.500"

.500"

RELIEVED FOR WELDING

.750" RAD.

.450"

.700"

.500"

1.00"

SIDE

REAR

Diagram #21

FRONT HINGE BLOCK

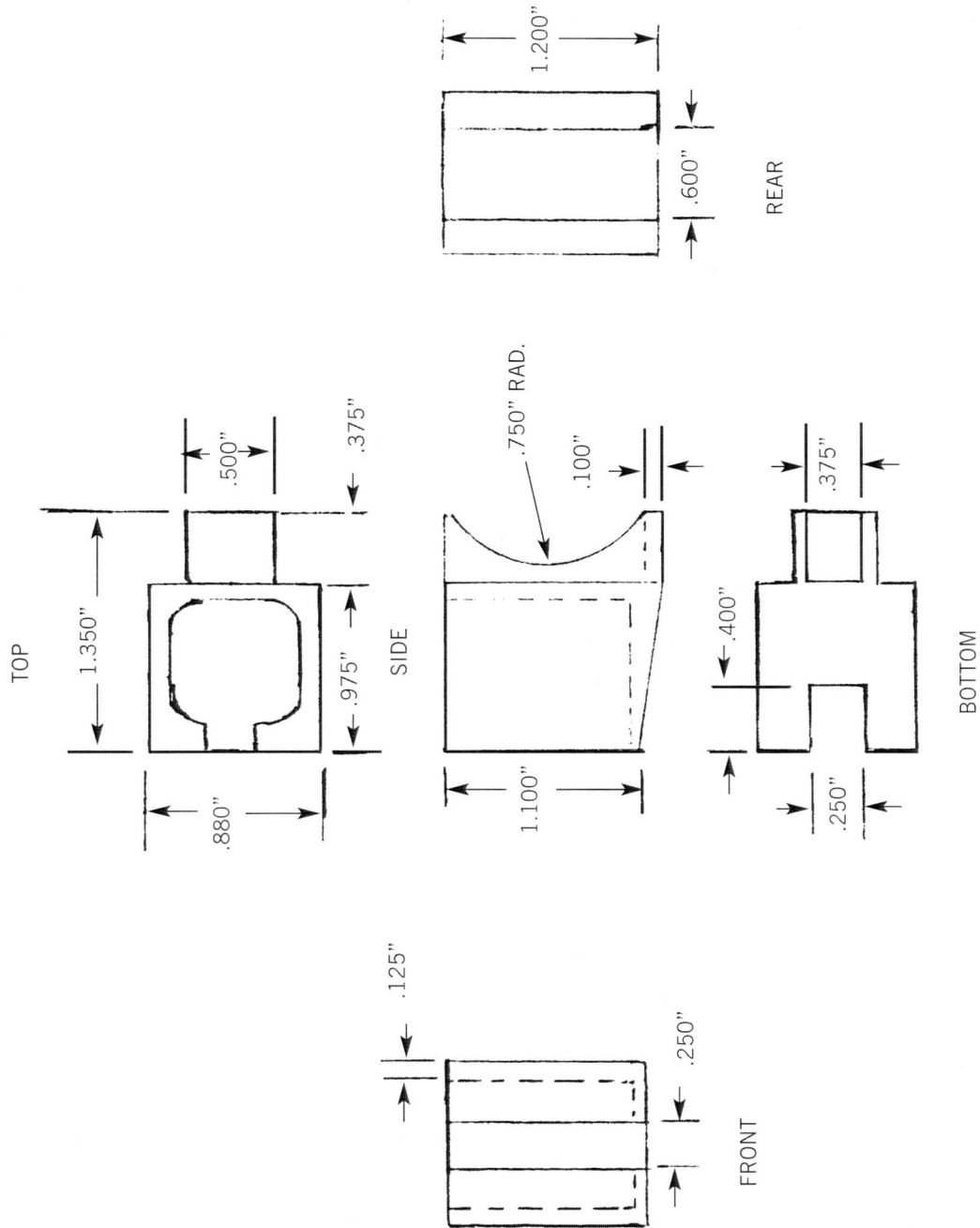

1.200"

.600"

REAR

.500"

.375"

TOP

1.350"

.880"

.975"

SIDE

.750" RAD.

.100"

1.100"

.375"

.400"

BOTTOM

.250"

.125"

.250"

FRONT

Diagram #22

Both sheet metal sections are clamped against form blocks in a large vise and formed with a heavy hammer. As I have stated before, the form block should be supported with blocks between the vise cross arm and bottom of the form block to prevent the work from being driven downward below the vise jaws while it is being formed with the hammer.

In practice the sheet metal blank is clamped against the form block with the material required to form one side projecting above the form block and vise jaws. The side thus extending is bent down against the form block. This done, the blank is turned over and again secured in the vise. The remaining side, now extending above the vise jaws and form block, is bent at a right angle as before. Both blanks are formed in the same manner.

The formed blanks are positioned at right angles to each other with the top edges even and in a straight line. If the short magazine version is used, three 1/4-inch holes are drilled through each side of the magazine box part, as shown. Both parts are clamped together with the form blocks in place. The vertical seams at the rear of the magazine box are welded, preferably by the TIG process, and the four holes welded shut. These should be built up above the surface and dressed back flush. if this is done properly, no evidence of the welds will show.

A rectangular block, 5/8″ x 7/8″ x 1 1/8″, is welded to the upper front side to form the front mounting pin base (hinge block). This block should be beveled deeply on the sides adjacent to the front face of the receiver to allow a heavy, deep weld joint. When this shop-made lower receiver is compared to an original receiver it will be noted that the mounting bracket, or front hinge pin base as it is sometimes known, is quite a bit larger and thicker. This will add a small amount of weight, but it also adds quite a lot of strength, making it well worthwhile as far as I am concerned.

A filler block is made up as shown in Diagram #22 to be welded in place at the rear of the magazine opening. The longer version is to be used with the pistol-caliber magazines and is made from 7/8-inch material. The inside has all the metal possible removed to save weight, and the rear portion is shaped to match the original as closely as possible. The long magazine version is made by welding a plate made from 12-gauge sheet metal across the back of the magazine opening and welding or silver-soldering a shaped filler block to this plate. This too is shaped to match the contour of the original as closely as possible.

The welded seams should be dressed smooth and flush with the surface wherever possible. This is done prior to installing the filler block at

the rear end of the receiver so that the receiver can be mounted in the milling machine without interference from protruding weld joints and the top side milled flat. The front block is cut back to the magazine opening with a 3/4-inch radius to match the upper receiver contour. A 1/2-inch slot, 5/8 inch deep, is cut in the center of the front block to accept the front mounting pin bracket of the upper receiver. Both receivers should now fit together closely. If they do not, check for high spots or burrs that are causing the interference and remove them.

Both receivers are clamped together and the front hinge pin hole is drilled through them simultaneously with a 7/32 (.2188)-inch drill (after locating and starting the hole with a center drill). This is followed by a 1/4-inch drill through one side only of the lower receiver and the upper bracket. The remaining smaller hole is tapped using a 1/4 x 28 tap. This is assuming that you will use the headless screws instead of pins to hold the assemblies together. Otherwise you should drill the hole completely through with the 1/4-inch drill, install the spring and detent to hold it in place, and use the standard push pin.

A filler block to be installed at the extreme rear of the receiver is cut from 7/8-inch steel plate to the shape and dimensions shown in Diagram #22. Here again, this part should match the contour of the original as closely as possible. As much material as possible should be cut from the inside of this part to reduce weight.

A round section, composed of the same material as the bolt(s) were made from, is turned to a diameter of 1.375 inches and an overall length of 1.350 inches. The inside is bored to a diameter of .990 and threaded with a 1.065-inch -by-16-TPI thread. This threaded sleeve is then clamped on the top side of the filler block and welded in place. The top edges of the filler block should have been beveled prior to welding, permitting a deeper, heavier weld joint. The resulting welds must be dressed back flush with the surface before the work proceeds further.

Magazine rear filler.

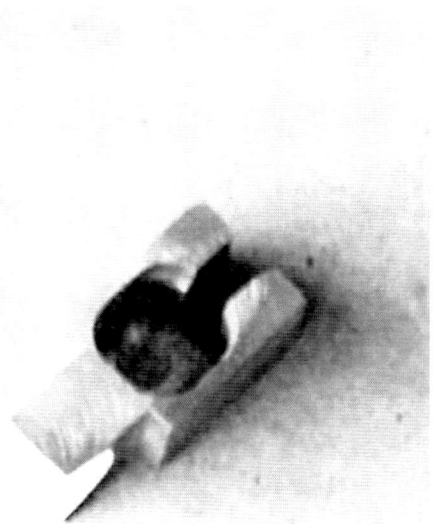

Inside is bored out to reduce weight.

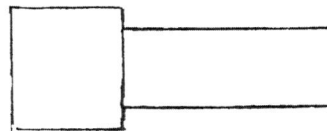

TOP VIEW

DRILL .217" TAP 1/4 x 28

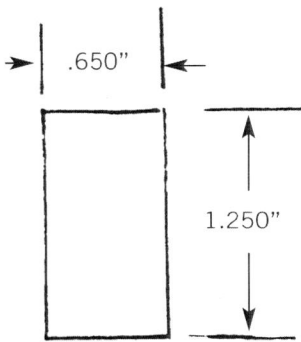

.650"

1.250"

FRONT VIEW

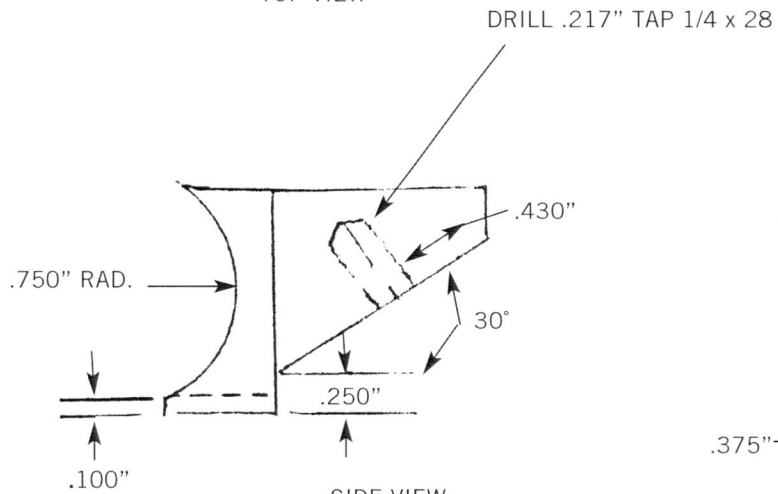

.750" RAD.

.430"

30°

.250"

.100"

.650"

.375"

SIDE VIEW

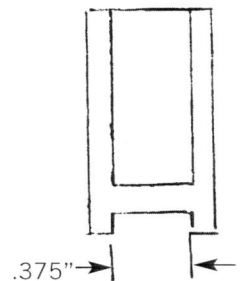

.375"

REAR

Diagram #23

GRIP MOUNTNG BRACKET AND REAR END OF TRIGGER GUARD

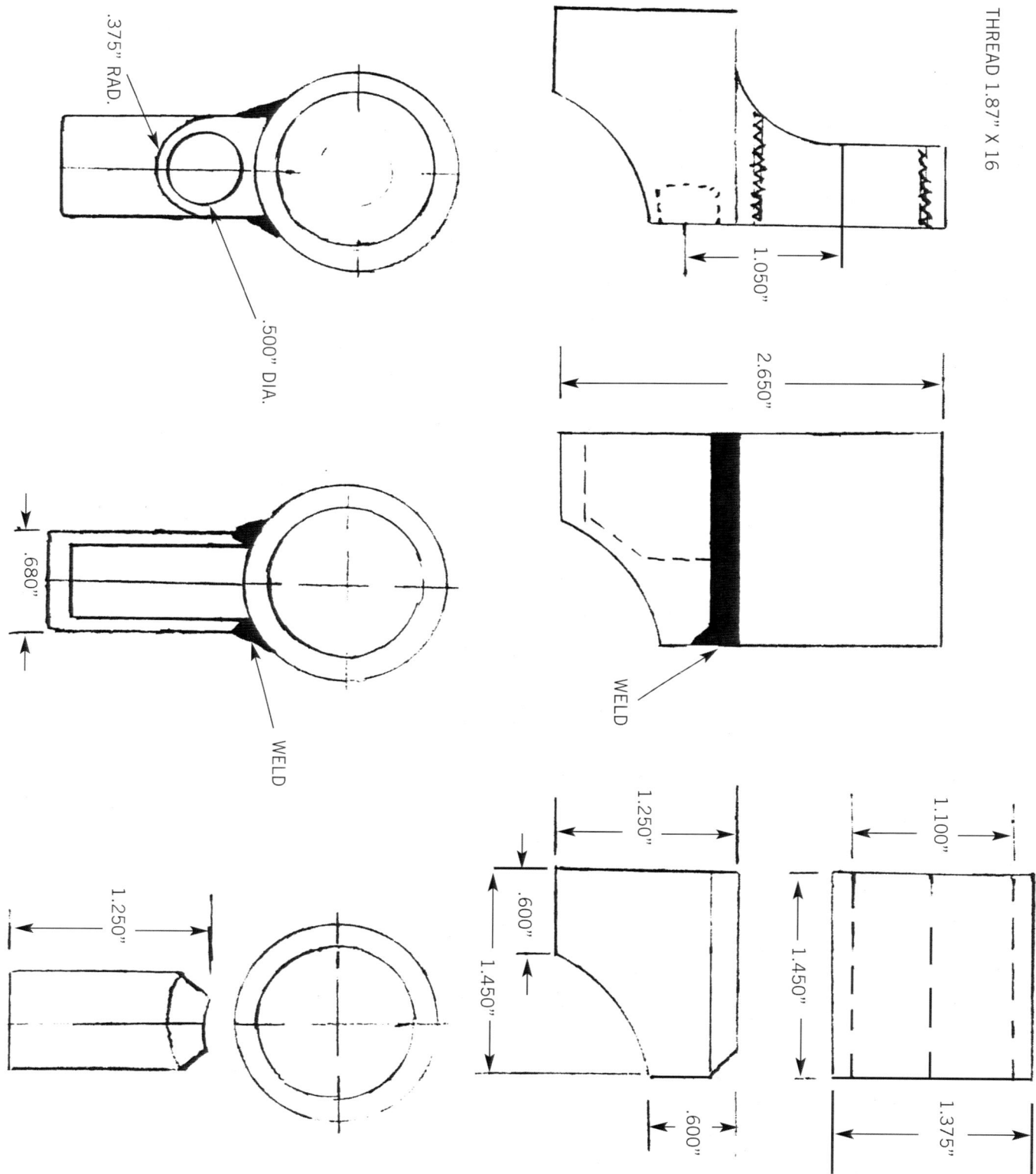

.375" RAD.

.500" DIA.

.680"

WELD

THREAD 1.87" X 16

1.050"

2.650"

WELD

1.250"

.600"

1.450"

.600"

1.100"

1.450"

1.375"

1.250"

Diagram #24

BUTT STOCK MOUNTING BRACKET

Ready to locate and weld in place.

When positioned correctly, magazine is a snug fit.

The front face of the cylindrical portion should be shaped to the same contour as the radiused lower rear end of the lower receiver. If this receiver is intended only for use with shop-made upper receivers, the exact contour is not important. The only requirement is that both parts mate closely. If, however, it is ever intended to be used with a commercial upper assembly, it is important that the 5/8-inch radius used on the commercial part be preserved. This can be formed rather simply using a 1 1/4-inch end mill. Such end mills, with a 3/4-inch-diameter shank to allow use in the more or less standard R8 collets, are expensive and many times hard to find, so other methods may be required to form it. If a rotary table is available it is a fairly simple matter to form the curve required. Otherwise, a fairly satisfactory job can be done by roughing it to shape using the largest milling cutter available and finishing it with a hand grinder and/or half round files. A hole for the tenon that keeps the stock from turning should be drilled as shown in the drawing before this part is welded in place. It is hard to locate and drill after installation.

To assure a close fit and proper alignment, a mandrel some 7 inches long is turned to just fit inside the upper receiver for at least 5 inches. The remainder is turned to a close fit inside the threaded cylindrical part of the lower. Both ends

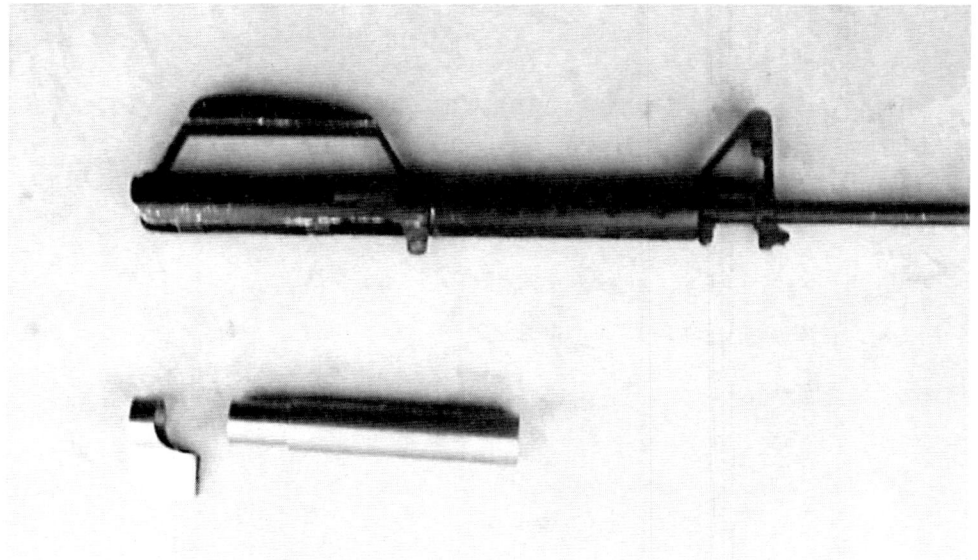

Mandrel is used to align parts for welding.

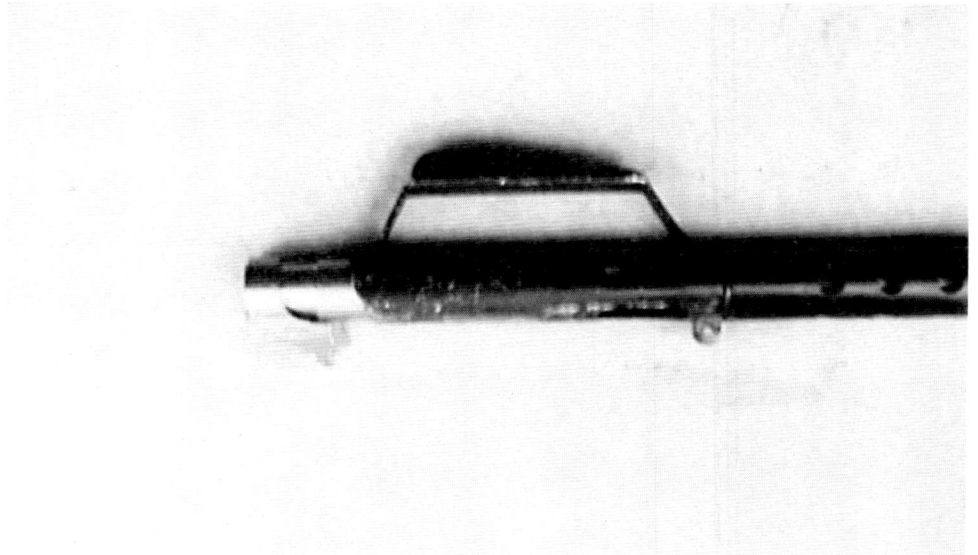

Mandrel is inserted in upper receiver with bracket in place on smaller end.

are drilled and tapped to accept 1/4 x 28 draw bolts to a depth of at least 1 inch. Large washers, big enough to fit over each end of the receiver openings, are required for each draw bolt.

The mandrel is installed inside the upper receiver, and the draw bolt—with washer in place—is screwed into the front end. The filler block is then pushed in place over the smaller end of the mandrel and the other draw

7.750"

1.540"

1.00"

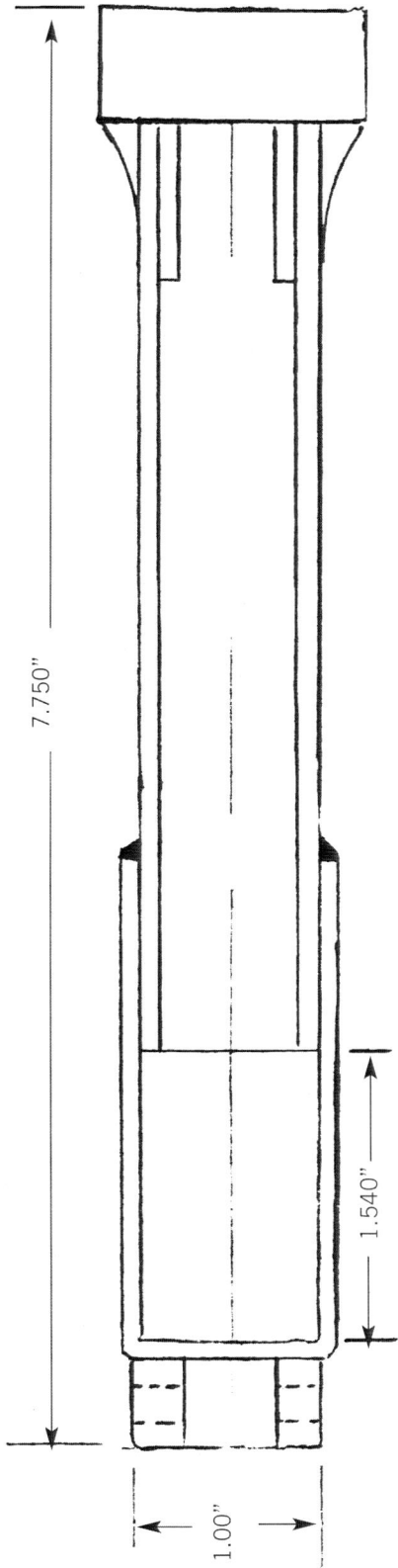

TOP VIEW, SHORT MAGAZINE

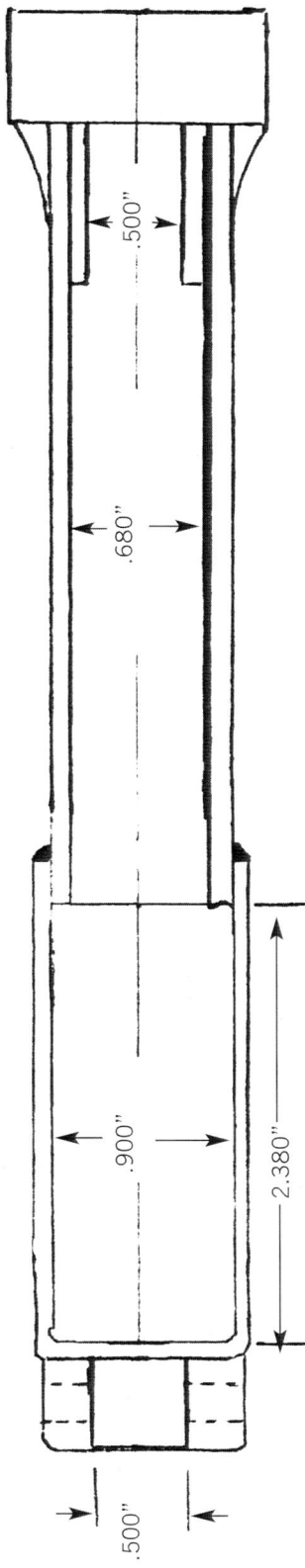

.500"

.680"

.900"

2.380"

.500"

TOP VIEW, FULL-LENGTH MAGAZINE

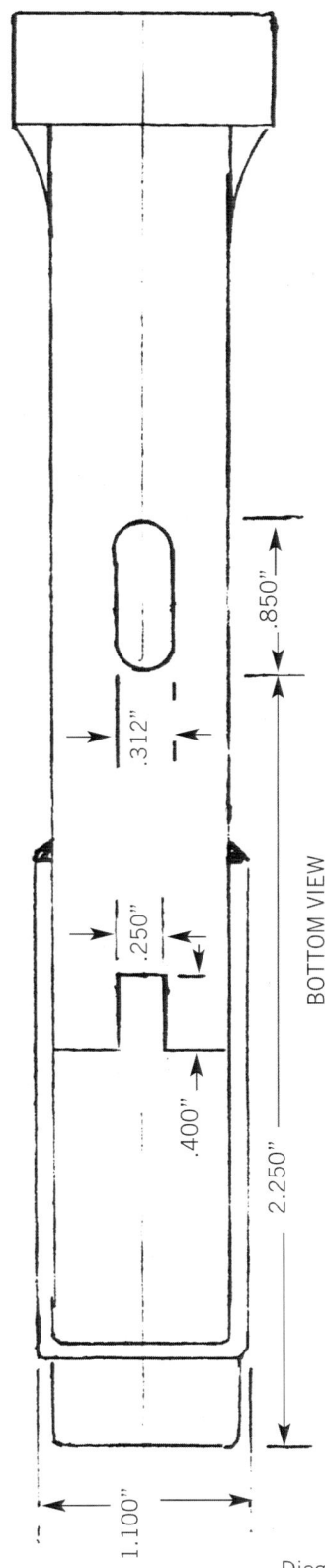

.850"

.312"

.250"

.400"

2.250"

1.100"

BOTTOM VIEW

LOWER RECEIVER

Diagram #25

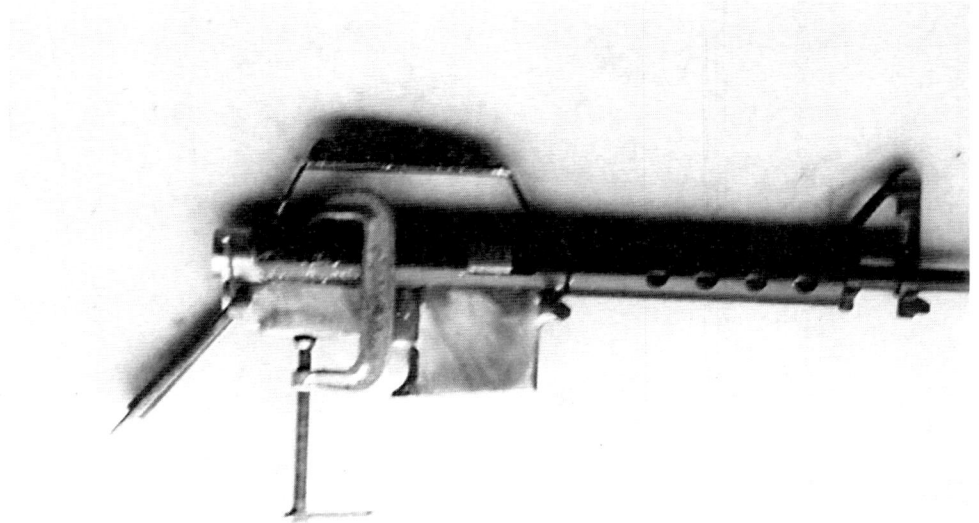

Clamped in place ready for welding to lower receiver.

bolt/washer installed and drawn up tight, pulling the two parts together as closely as possible. The assembly is put in place on the lower receiver and the sheet metal trimmed to expose enough of the filler block to assure an ample weld seam.

When this is accomplished, the front hinge pin is installed and both parts are clamped together at the rear. The filler block is now welded in place along both sides under the round portion and completely around the back and along the lower sides. The parts should be allowed to cool before the clamp, hinge pin, and mandrel are removed to minimize any chances of warpage.

If desired, the trigger guard can be hinged as on the original, but an equally satisfactory guard can be made by slotting the front and rear of the guard uprights and silver-soldering a sheet metal strap in place.

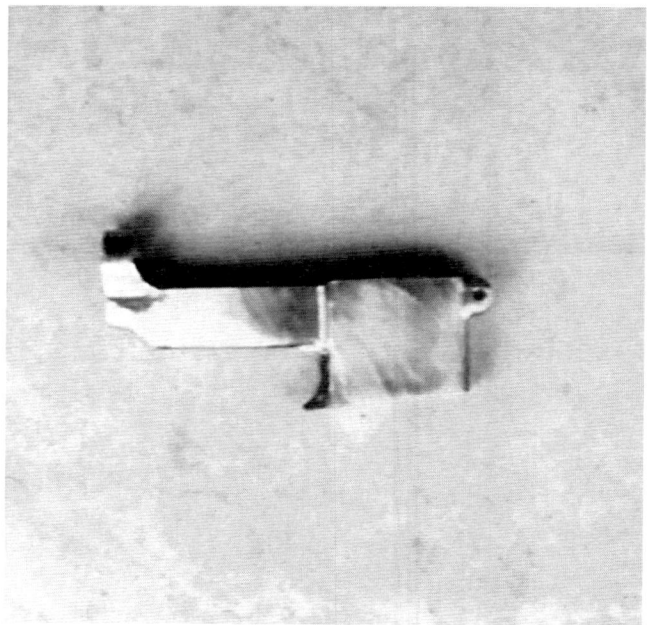

Welding completed and rough-finished.

Rear trigger guard and grip mount.

Bottom view of rear trigger guard.

Rear guard welded in place.

At this point all weld joints should be dressed smooth and the entire assembly should be polished, smooth, and free of tool marks. Next the assembly is secured in the milling machine vise, making certain that it is flat and level and square with the table. Now, using the dimensions given in the drawing, the various holes are located and drilled. This can be done with complete accuracy through use of the graduated dials on both the longitudinal and cross feeds. Using the front edge of the magazine well and the top of the receiver as starting points, the work is moved to the correct location for the hammer pin hole and the hole is drilled. As usual, it should be started with a center drill, followed by an undersized drill and then the full-size drill. Holes drilled using this method are not as likely to deflect or crawl, as is common when only the full-size drill is used. The work is then moved to the correct location for the next hole and drilled using the same method. This is repeated until all are drilled. A slot is cut in the location shown for the trigger and a hole for the grip bolt drilled and tapped.

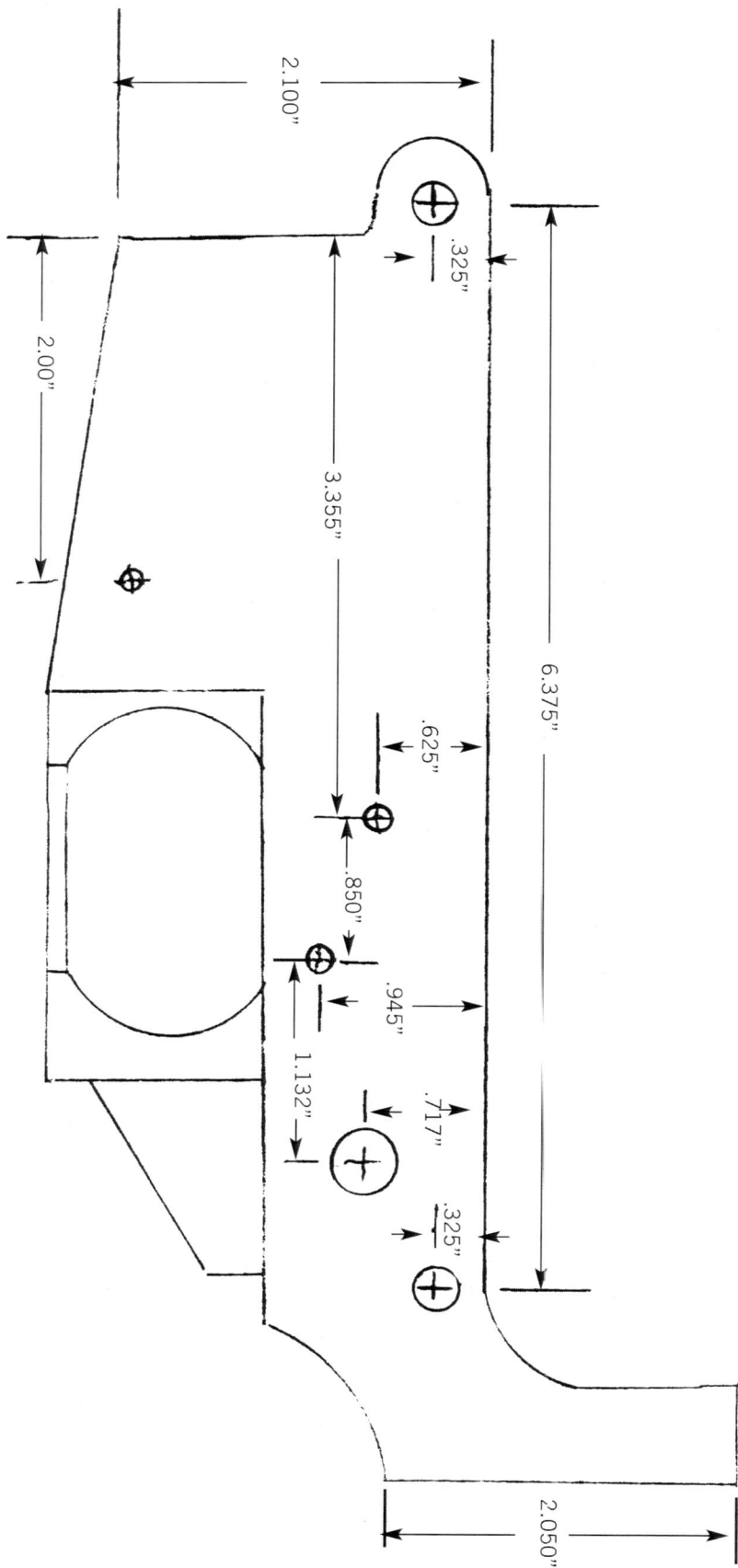

LOWER RECEIVER HOLE LOCATIONS

2.100"

2.00"

3.355"

6.375"

.325"

.625"

.850"

.945"

1.132"

.717"

.325"

2.050"

Diagram #26

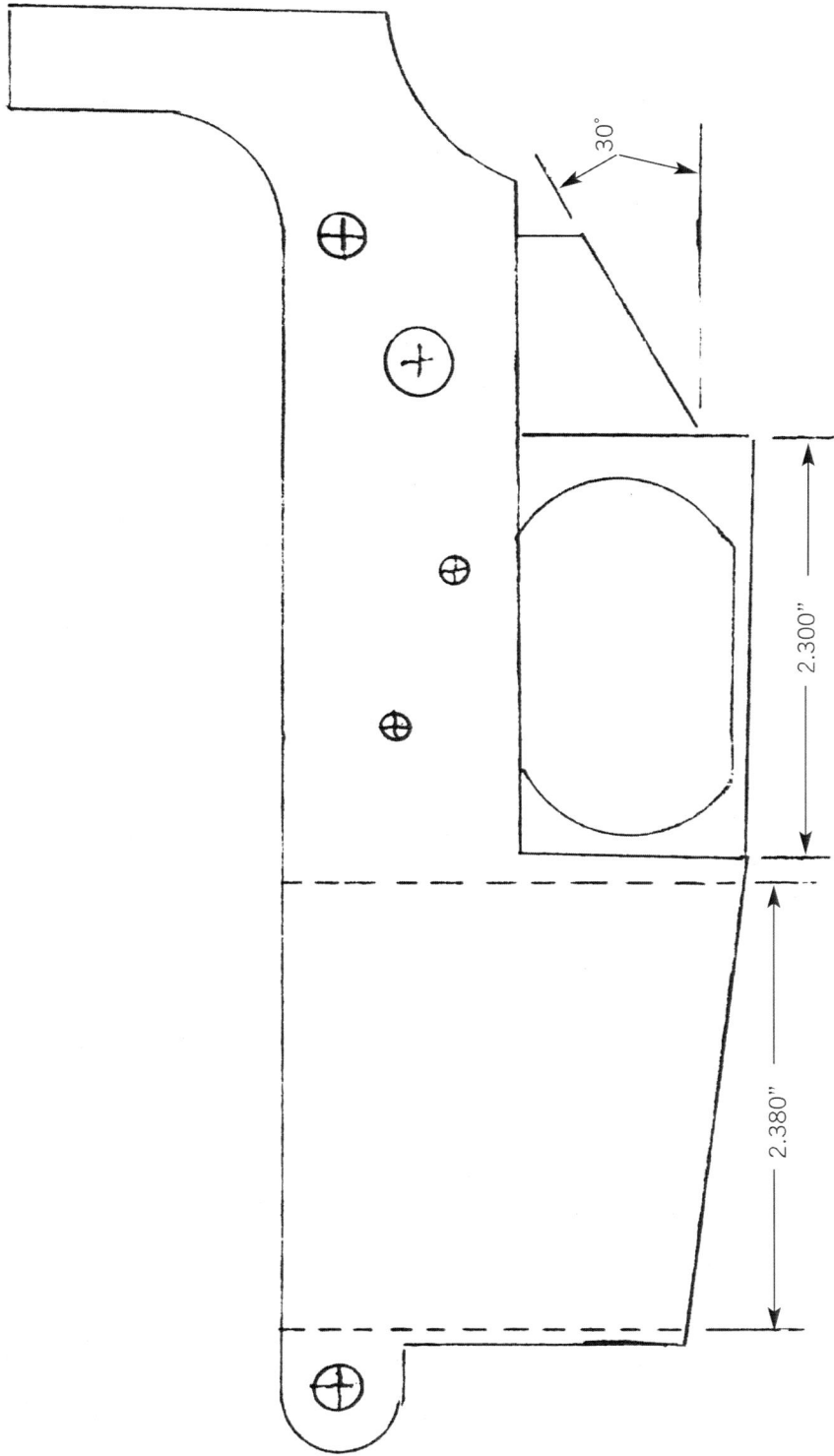

30°

2.300"

2.380"

LOWER RECEIVER WITH FULL-LENGTH MAGAZINE

Diagram #27

While the operations described may seem time-consuming and complicated, it isn't actually as difficult as it may seem. Such a receiver will require a full day's work to build from start to finish, but if one wants one bad enough and this is the only way to get it, it will be worthwhile.

Again, be advised that this part may be illegal to manufacture. Think carefully and weigh the consequences before you build one. Mine was made before the so-called "assault weapons" ban went into effect and is therefore considered legal. But since the law is now in effect, I wouldn't be interested in building another. The requirement that home-manufactured firearms be marked with the maker's name, address, and a serial number should also be kept in mind.

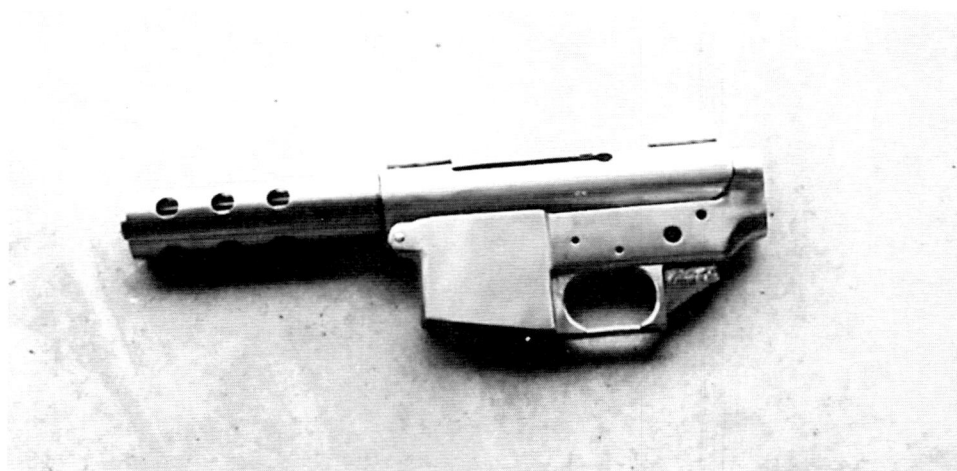

Completed lower receiver with pistol version upper pinned in place.

Lower receiver with open bolt plug partially inserted.

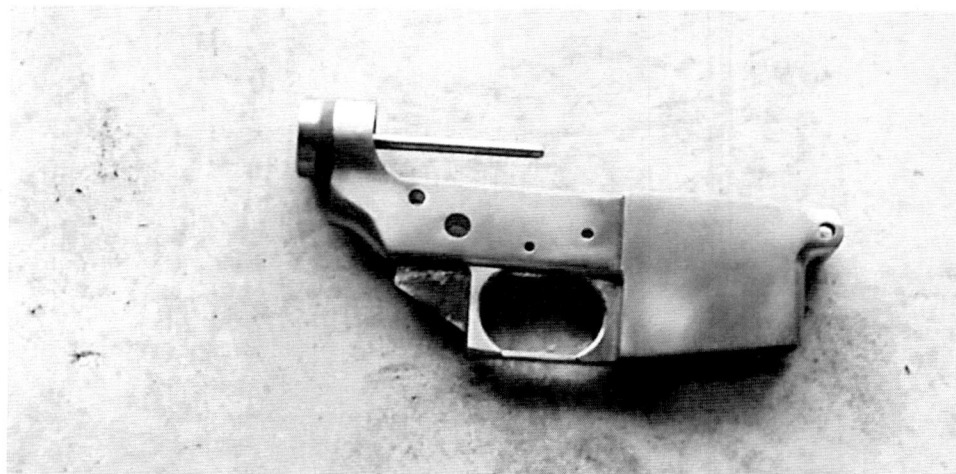

Same, with breech plug in place.

Male and female dies used to form offset in left receiver wall of full-length magazine opening.

Offset partially formed, further clamping pressure will finish.

Clamping pressure can be exerted using sturdy vise with extension on vise handle. Don't try this with a cheap import vise.

View of offset, formed as shown.

MAGAZINES

For years many of us used Sten magazines in our experimental assault-type firearms, mainly because they were plentiful and cheap. Apparently they are still plentiful, although the price has gone up.

While the existing magazines should probably be used as long as they are available, mainly to save labor, an alternate source of supply should be kept in mind. This means making them yourself. Although I have detailed a method for making them in other books, a different method, which is somewhat easier but equally satisfactory when properly done, is described herein.

It should be pointed out that this unit was originally designed as a 9mm conversion only, to mate with existing AR-15 or M16 lower receiver assemblies. The Sten magazine is the correct width to just fit inside the original magazine well, and, when used in combination with the magazine adapter described in the small parts chapter, allows a close, snug fit. If the unit is built in one of the 10mm calibers or .45 ACP, the same outside dimensions must be adhered to since wider magazines, such as the Thompson, grease gun, and the like, will not go in the hole.

The same Sten magazines as used in the 9mm can be used with the larger calibers if the inside is simply swaged slightly longer to permit feeding of the longer cartridges. The maximum overall length of the .45 ACP cartridge is stated to be 1.275 inches, and that of the 10mms is somewhat less, depending on which one is used. All that is required is to swage the concave seam at the rear of the magazine body slightly flat, thereby lengthening the inside of the body without increasing the outside length.

The swage used to accomplish this is made from a flat bar of steel 1.300 inches wide, .312 inch thick, and 11 inches long. The .312 (5/16)-inch width is to permit the swage to pass between the magazine lips. The 11-inch length is to allow each end of the swage to extend from the body so that each end can be supported on blocks while any deformation caused by the swaging operation is restored to its original shape using a block and hammer. The end intended to enter the magazine body should have a short bevel on all four edges.

In use, the swage should be lubricated with heavy grease and started into the bottom end of the magazine body. A steel spacer, .187 (3/16) inch thick and 1 inch wide, is positioned on each side of the swage to keep it in place under the seam. It is forced into the magazine body by light hammer blows. When completely through and extending past the feed lips, the swage is supported at each end by steel blocks and the back side restored to its original flat shape using a block and hammer. The magazine lips must be spread open slightly to facilitate feeding of the thicker cartridge. This is accomplished using

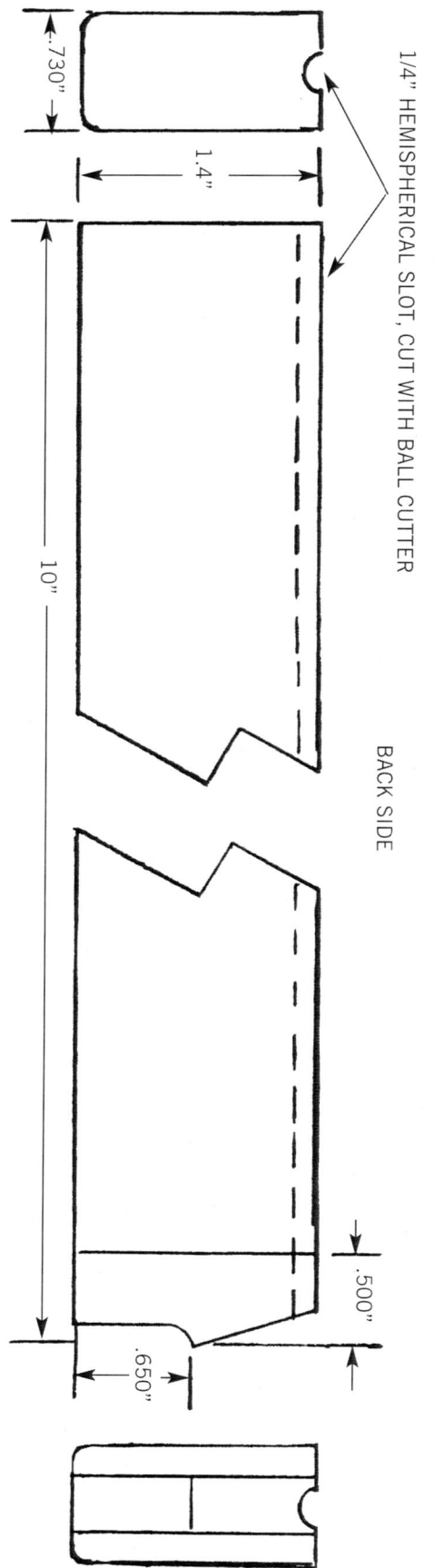

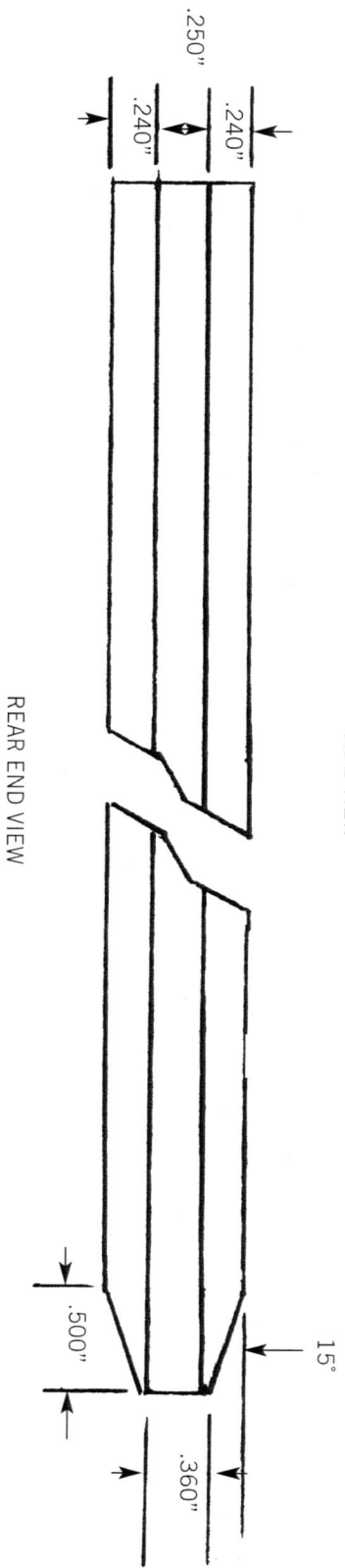

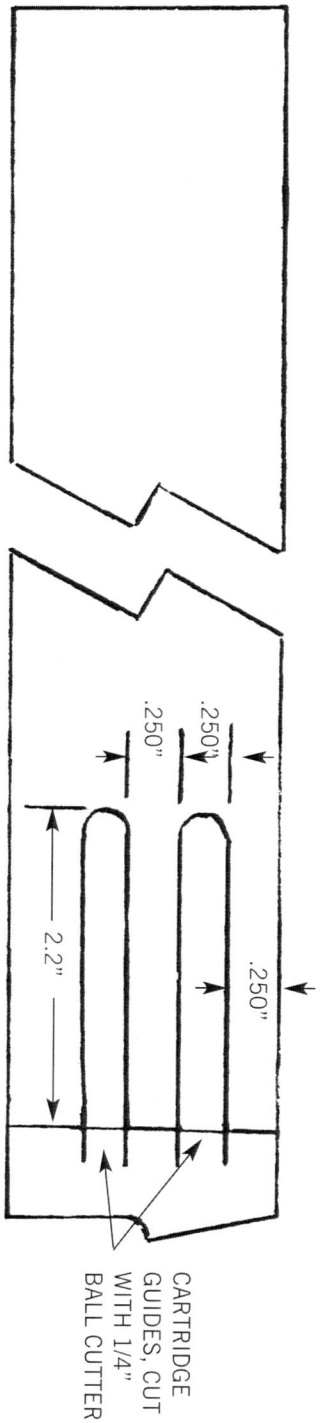

MAGAZINE FORM BLOCK

1/4" HEMISPHERICAL SLOT, CUT WITH BALL CUTTER

BACK SIDE

.730"

1.4"

10"

.500"

.650"

SIDE VIEW

.250"

.240"

.240"

.500"

15°

.360"

REAR END VIEW

.250"

.250"

.250"

2.2"

CARTRIDGE
GUIDES, CUT
WITH 1/4"
BALL CUTTER

Diagram #28

74

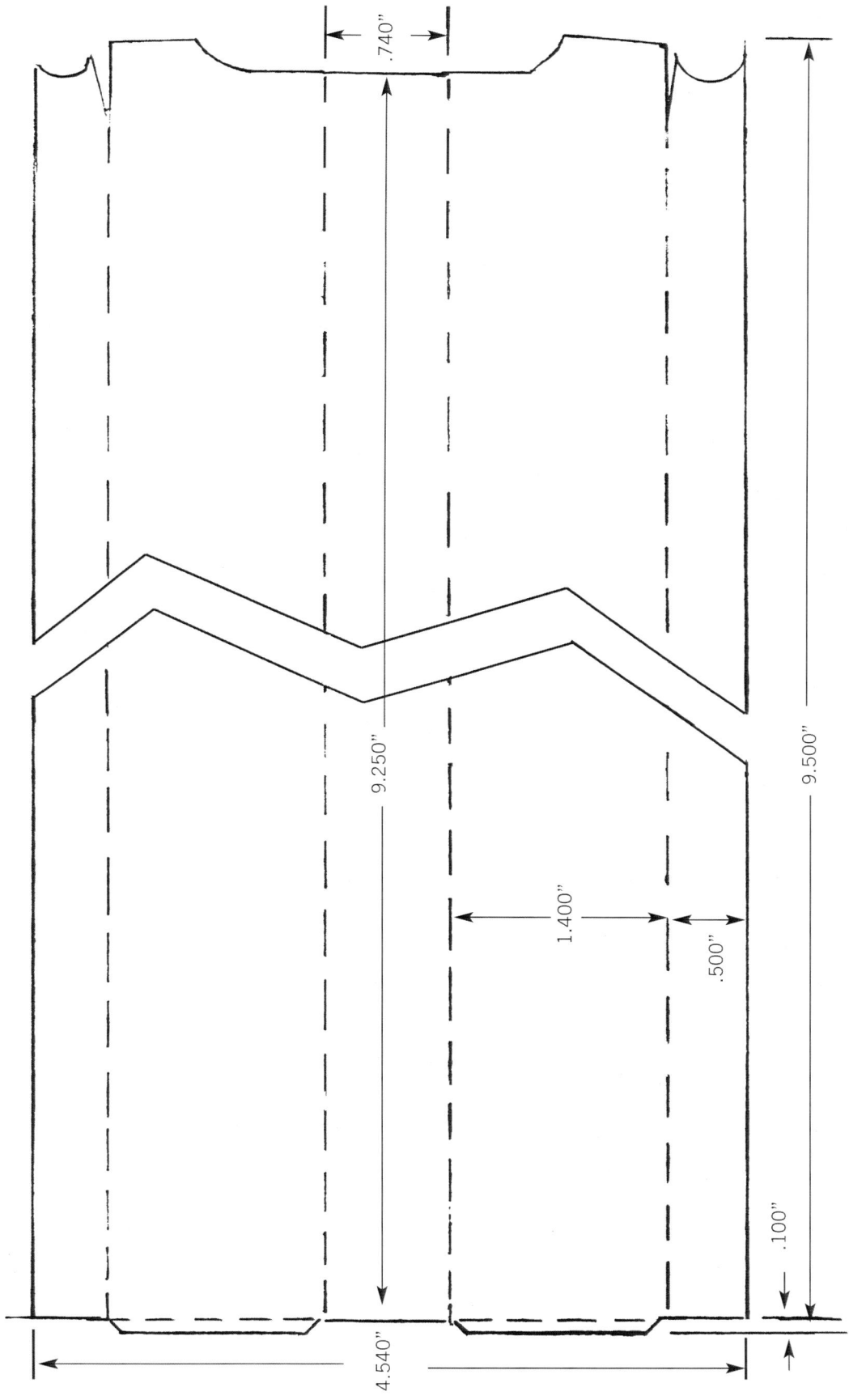

.740"

9.250"

9.500"

1.400"

.500"

.100"

4.540"

MAGAZINE BODY PATTERN

Diagram #29

75

pliers or vise grips and is more or less a trial-and-error operation.

Sten magazines reworked in this fashion will hold eighteen to twenty .45 rounds or twenty-three to twenty-five rounds of 10mm ammunition. Lesser-capacity magazines can be made by cutting and reducing the length of an original magazine and rebending the flanges at the bottom for the floorplate to slide over. Needless to say, the follower spring is shortened by a corresponding amount. The follower legs can be shortened by as much as 3/4 inch with no ill effect, thus allowing a shorter magazine while retaining a larger capacity.

New magazines can be manufactured by making up a form block and bending the sheet metal body around it. The form block should be 1.400 inches deep, .730 inch wide and 10 inches long. This can be made from a solid bar or from thinner strips welded or riveted together. It is a fairly simple matter to reduce a bar of 1 1/2" x 3/4" material to size, just as it is to fasten three

1/4" x 1 1/2" strips together and cut them down in the same manner. The corners on the front side should be rounded to approximately a 1/8-inch radius. The rear corners should be fairly sharp, radiused only slightly. A convex slot is cut along the centerline on the back side of the block. This slot should have a .125-inch radius and can be cut with a 1/4-inch ball-cutting end mill to a depth of .100 inch if for a .45 magazine and .150 inch if intended for a 9mm. The end that will form the top, or lip end, should be cut at a 5-degree angle by 1/2 inch long.

Two more concave grooves with a .125-inch radius must be cut on each side at the top as shown in Diagram #30. These form guide ribs, which will assist in the reduction of the staggered, near double-row magazine to the single-row feeding, which, at least in my opinion, is far superior to a double-row feed. A 1/8-inch hole is drilled on center near each end and on the front side of the block, and close-fitting guide pins are installed.

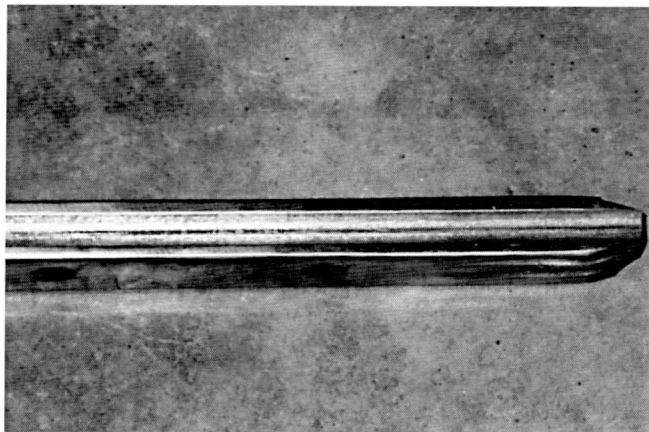

Groove is cut on rear side of form block using ball cutter.

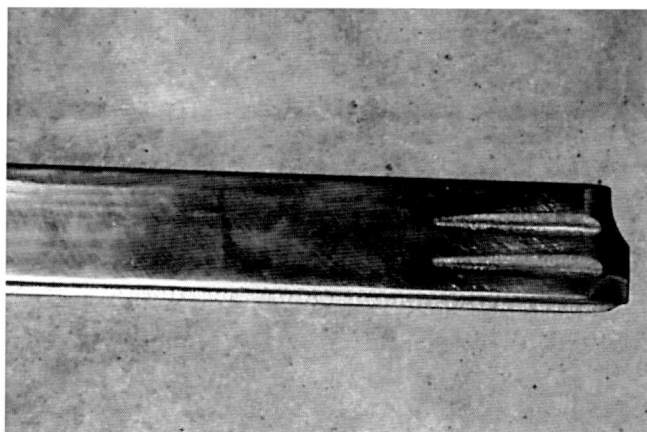

Cuts to form guide ribs are made with same ball cutter.

FLOORPLATE

1.300"

.500"

1.6800"

1.050"

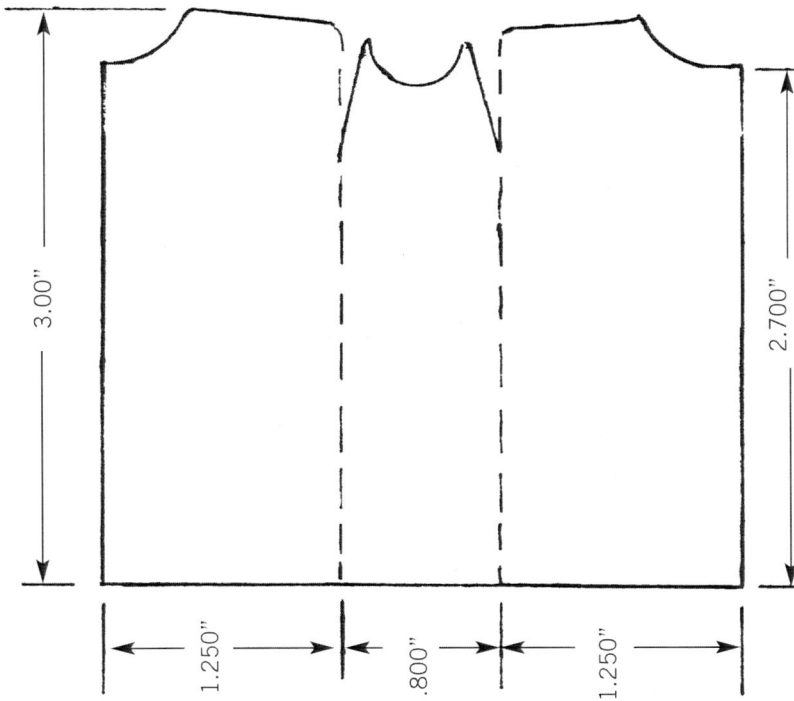

UPPER REINFORCING JACKET

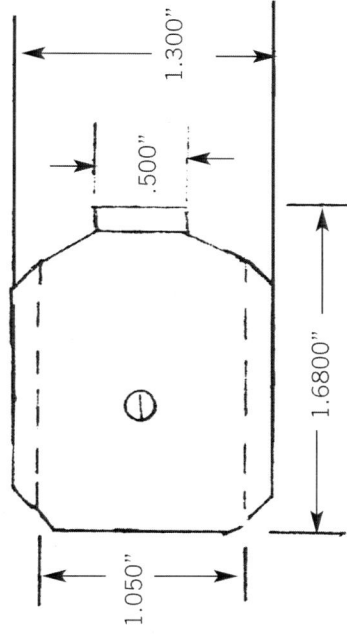

3.00"

2.700"

1.250"

.800"

1.250"

Diagram #30

It will be noted that the sides of original factory-made magazines have a slight taper toward the front. This is omitted with the shop-made units since the taper is difficult to form using the method described here. If the guide ribs and magazine lips are formed correctly, no deleterious effect will result.

A blank is cut from 20-gauge (.032-inch) sheet metal to the dimensions shown with a centerline marked lengthwise. Corresponding holes to fit over the guide pins in the form block are drilled on the centerline. The blank is now mated to the block and the assembly clamped in the vise with the front and back surfaces between the vise jaws and the upper side of the block even with or slightly above the vise jaw. The underside should be blocked up using spacer blocks between the vise throat and bottom of the block. The protruding sheet metal is bent flat against the form block using a hammer and flat bar of metal. The assembly is then turned over and the other side bent flat in the same manner. An additional spacer must be added at the back for this last side to clear the previously bent side, which now extends past the surface of the block.

Template can be cemented to sheet metal as a guide to cutting magazine blank.

Form block and sheet metal blank are clamped in vise.

Sides are folded using block and hammer.

Rear sides are folded and formed using hammer and swage.

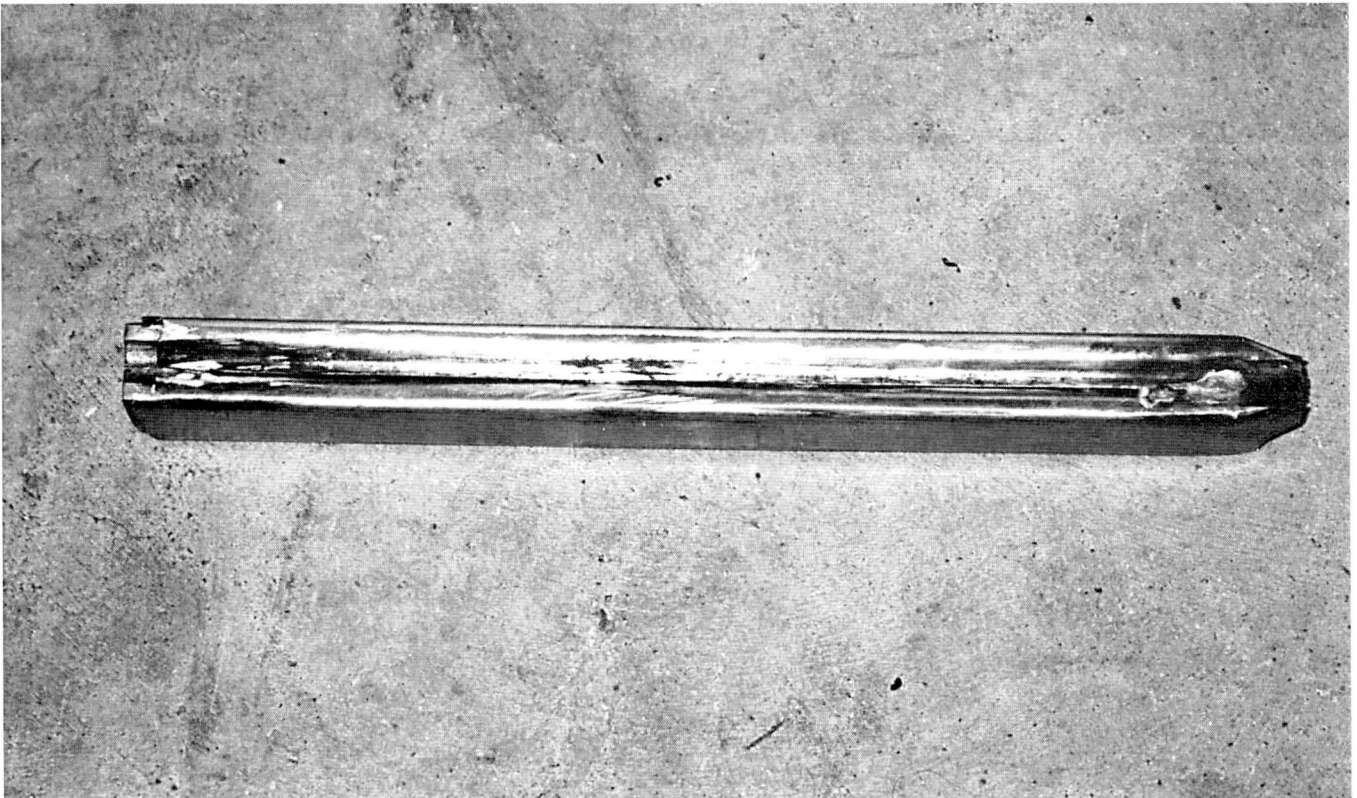

Seam is silver-soldered while clamped around form block.

The assembly is next turned with the front side down and again clamped in the vise and one side bent flat. The edge of this side is swaged in to the half round slot using a hammer and the rounded edge of a 3/16-inch-wide steel block. The remaining side is given the same treatment. At this point the seam is welded or silver-soldered. The magazine lips are bent flat against the form block and the guide ribs formed using the same 3/16-inch swage and hammer.

The upper "jacket" or collar is cut from the same 20-gauge sheet metal and mounted in place. If a number of small 3/16-inch holes are drilled through the sides of the jacket, the jacket can be welded to the body through these holes and the welds dressed flush. A neat appearance is thus preserved. The seams at the upper corners where the magazine lips are formed are also welded and the welds dressed flush.

A flange is bent outward at a right angle to the body at the bottom edge of each side. These are to hold the floorplate, which is cut from the same 20-gauge sheet metal and the edges bent to slip over the flanges. A hole to accept a pin that keeps the plate in place is drilled as shown in Diagram #30. The retaining strip, consisting of a 20-gauge sheet metal strip with both ends bent upward 90 degrees, is fabricated, and a hole corresponding to the one in the floorplate is drilled and a close-fitting pin silver-soldered in place. This serves to hold the floorplate in place except when the pin is pushed inward against pressure exerted by the magazine spring, which will allow the floorplate to be moved forward off the magazine. This permits removal of the magazine spring and follower.

While it is possible to

Rear sides are folded and formed using hammer and swage.

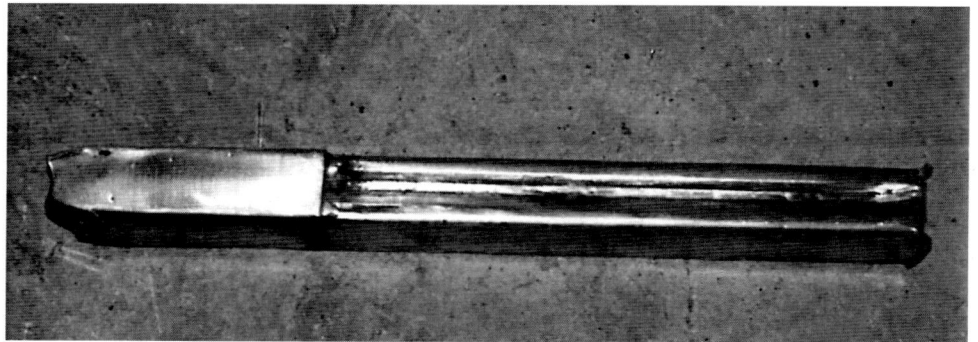

Upper jacket in place on magazine body.

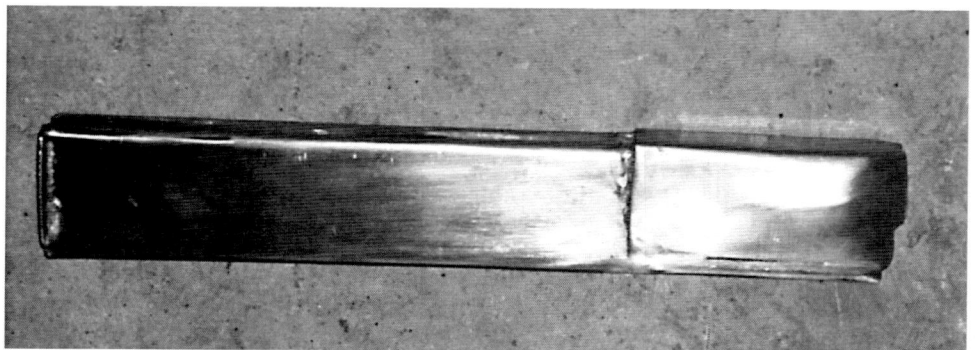

Upper jacket welded in place.

Upper end of magazine showing double wall thickness.

Magazine with cartridge in place, ready for feeding.

Lower end showing cover plate in place.

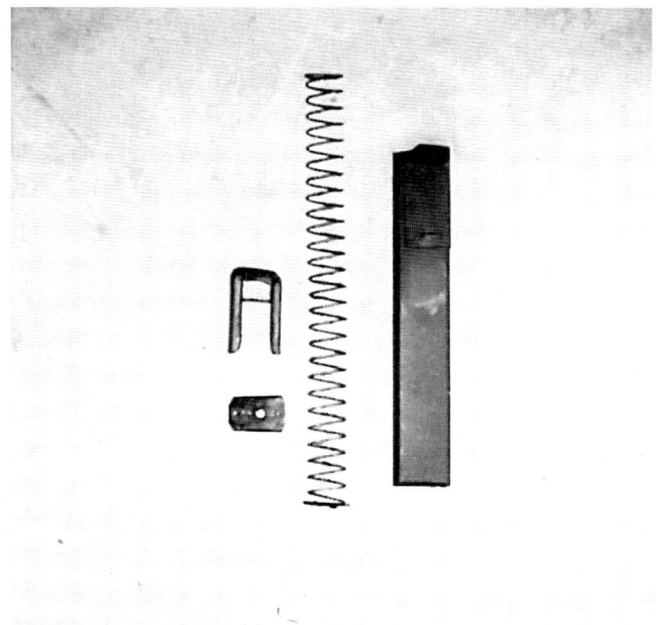

Component parts of factory magazine.

bend a magazine spring to shape using pliers, a much neater job will result when it is wound around a mandrel. This is accomplished by rounding the edges of a 3/8″ x 1″ steel bar, 14 inches long. A hole is drilled through the side at one end to accept .065-inch-diameter spring wire. The resulting mandrel is chucked in the lathe with the opposite end supported by the tail stock center. A V-shaped groove is cut across the faces of two small blocks that are clamped in the tool post. In practice, one end of a length of .065-inch-diameter music wire is passed through the V grooves of the tool post blocks and the extending end inserted in the hole in the mandrel. The tool post is tightened to exert tension against the wire as it is drawn through the notches. With the lathe running at the slowest speed and set for the coarsest thread

available, the spring is wound. The factory spring is approximately 13 inches long and consists of 26 coils spaced 1/2 inch apart. This should be duplicated as closely as possible.

The follower is made with a top section shaped as shown in Diagram #31, with a leg welded to each end. The magazine is assembled by first inserting the follower into the bottom end. The spring is then put in place, followed by the retaining strip. This retaining strip is depressed against the spring, and the floorplate is slipped over the flanges and pushed to the rear until the retainer pin snaps in place.

It is hoped that commercial magazines remain available and plentiful. If not, however, this need not present a major problem since, as can be seen here, satisfactory magazines can be made in the home workshop if necessary.

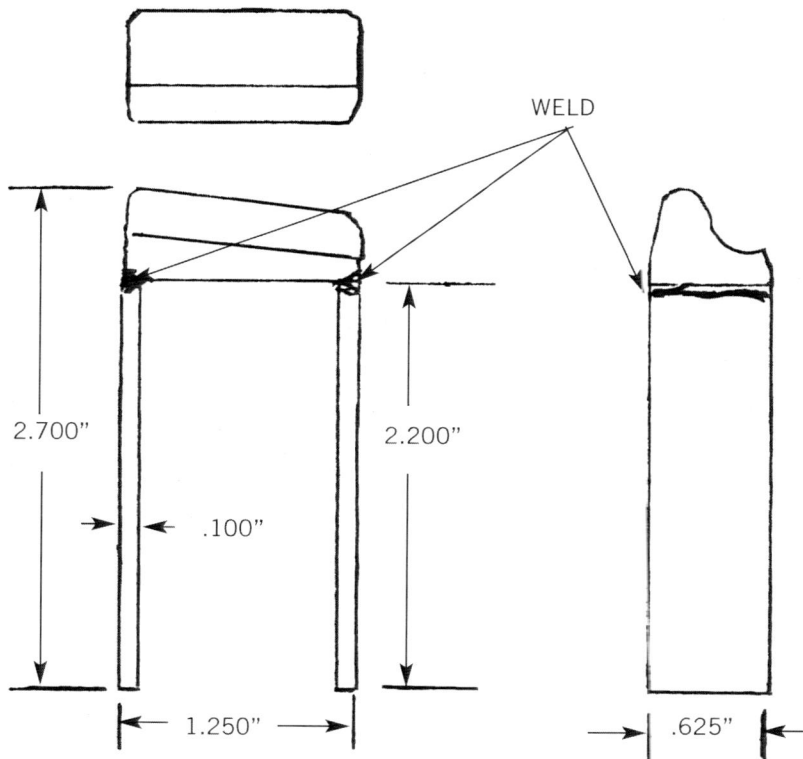

WELD

2.700"

2.200"

.100"

1.250"

.625"

Diagram #31   **MAGAZINE FOLLOWER**

SMALL PARTS

If an original lower receiver is used, a spacer, or filler block, which also serves as a mounting point for the magazine latch as well as the ejector, must be used. This part also serves to adapt the magazine opening to the size required to contain the smaller pistol cartridge magazine.

The block proper should be made from aluminum, not only to save weight but because it is also easier to machine than steel (usually). This part should fit the magazine opening closely. While approximate dimensions are given in in Diagram #32, these may not be anywhere close to the actual size required to fit your particular lower receiver since different manufacturers use different dimensions. This was the primary reason my commercially produced conversion units were not as successful as they should have been. If I made the filler block to maximum dimensions, my customers complained because of the work involved in filing them down to fit. On the other hand, if this part was made to fit the smaller, tighter opening found in another brand of lower receiver, enough sideways travel was introduced to prevent the ejector from working. So make this part to fit snug inside your magazine opening, so that it requires a slight effort to push it into place.

With the part properly fitted and in place, a slot for the original magazine latch to engage and hold this part in position should be marked through the existing slot in the lower receiver and cut with a 3/16-inch end mill.

A slot to accept the ejector is cut using a 1/8-inch end mill at the location shown in the drawing, and the ejector is cut to shape from 10-gauge flat stock. With the ejector in place, two 3/32-inch holes are drilled through both the block and the ejector simultaneously at the locations

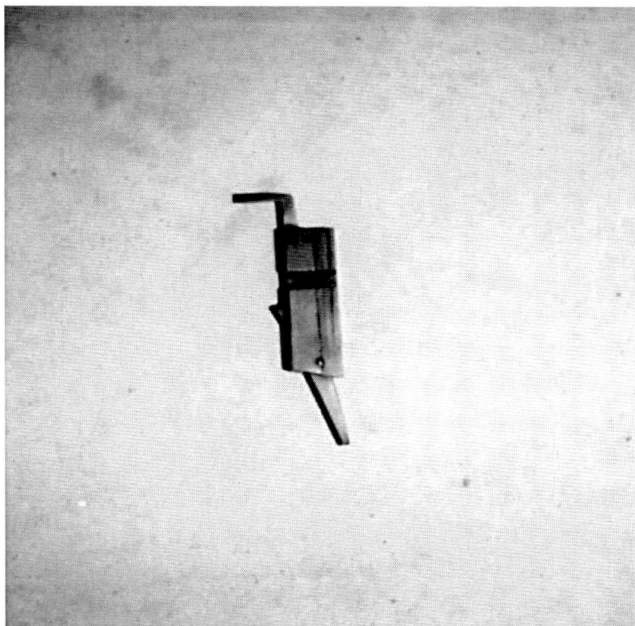

Magazine adapter for use with commercial receiver.

EXTRACTOR FORMED FROM .125"
HEAT-TREATABLE FLAT STOCK

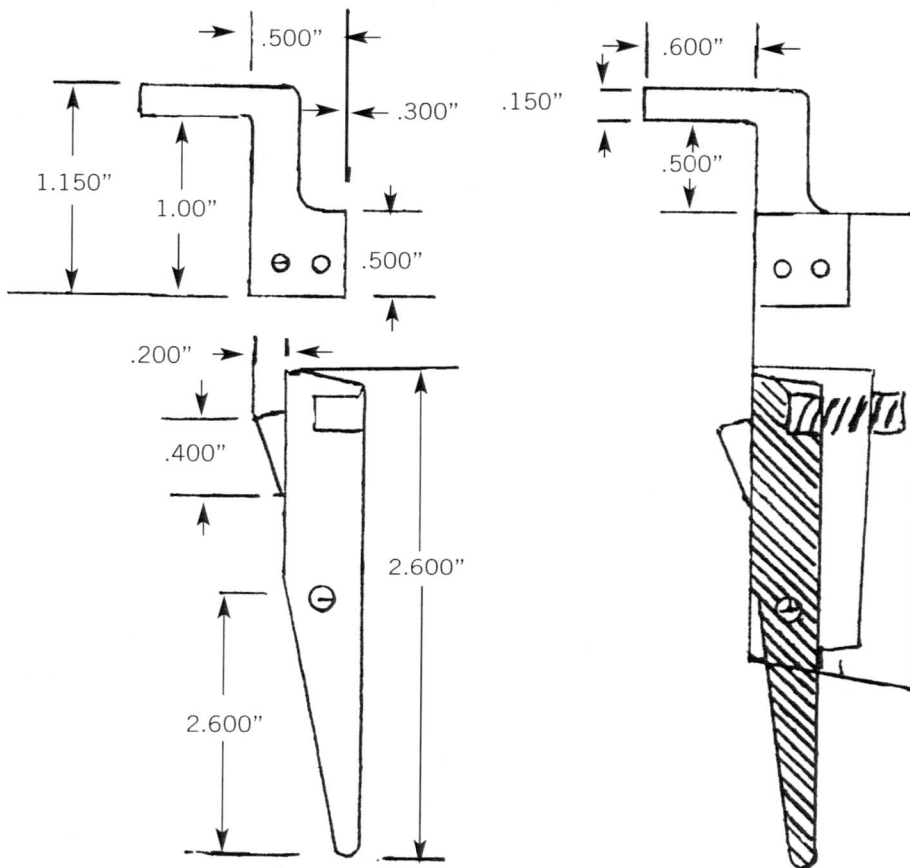

.500"

.300"

.150"

.600"

1.150"

1.00"

.500"

.500"

.200"

.400"

2.600"

2.600"

Diagram #32

MAGAZINE ADAPTOR COMPONENTS

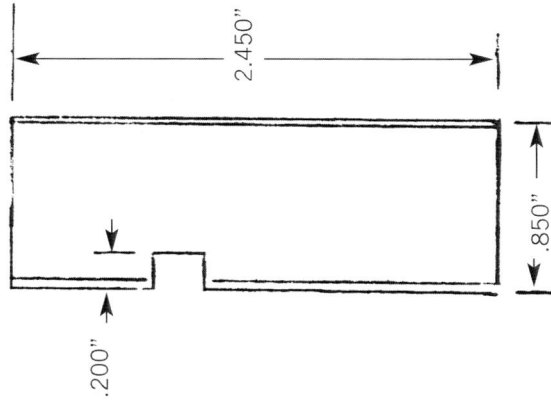

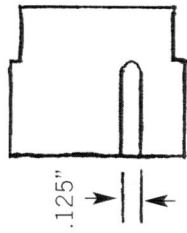

TOP

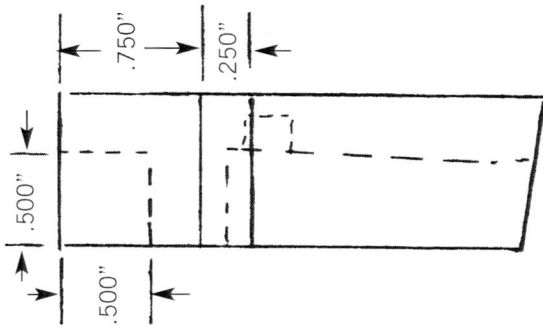

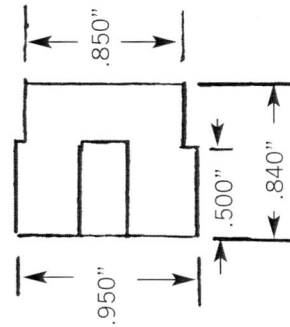

SIDE

BOTTOM

REAR

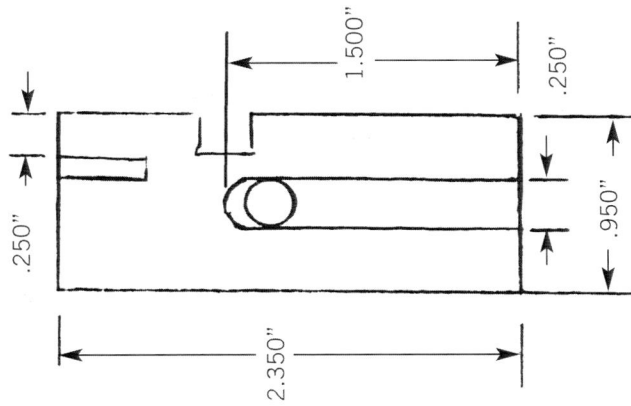

FRONT

MAGAZINE ADAPTOR USED WITH COMMERCIAL LOWER RECEIVER

Diagram #33

85

MAGAZINE LATCH, SHOP-MADE RECEIVER

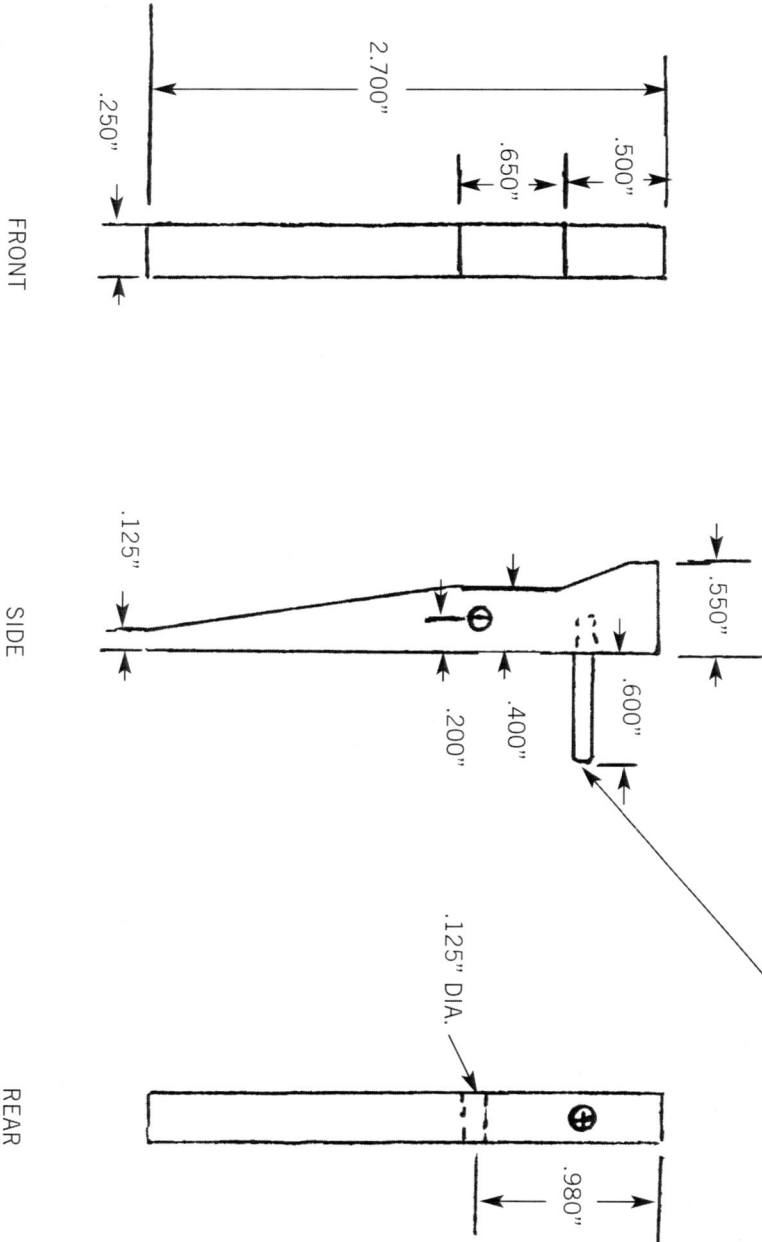

FRONT

2.700"

.250"

.650"

.500"

SIDE

.125"

.550"

.200"

.400"

.600"

.125" SPRING GUIDE SILVER-SOLDERED IN PLACE.

REAR

.125" DIA.

.980"

Diagram #34

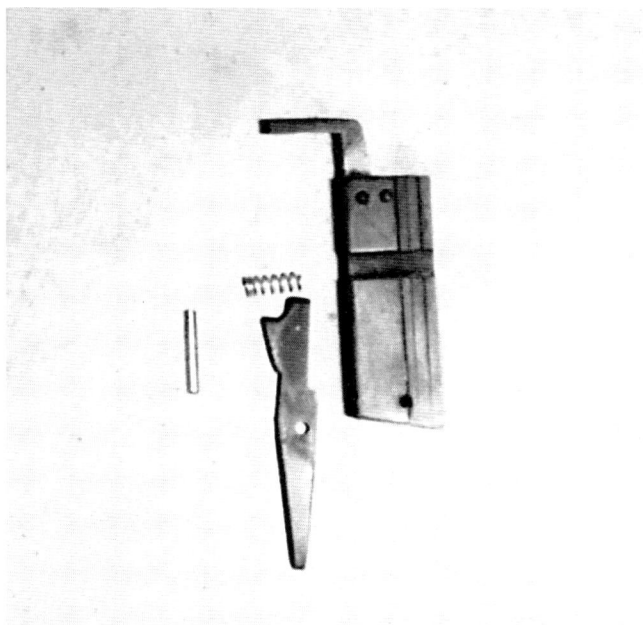

Component parts used in adapter.

Rear receiver-mounting bracket.

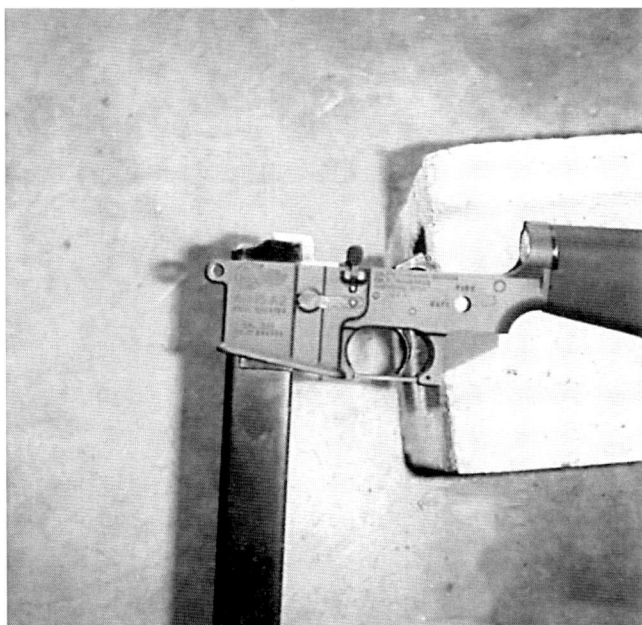

Adapter in place. (Note that original magazine latch limits depth of magazine insertion.)

shown, after which close-fitting pins are pressed in the holes to hold the ejector in place.

The magazine latch is cut to shape from 1/4-inch flat stock. The slot and spring pocket are milled in the front face of the block, and the pivot pin hole is drilled through both parts—again, simultaneously. The latch should be made slightly longer than shown in Diagram #34 to allow for proper fitting during assembly.

It should be obvious that if the shop-made receiver with the short magazine opening is used, the filler block is not used and the alternate magazine latch shown is used instead. The same sheet metal ejector is used; however, the slot to accept it is milled into the receiver and the part silver-soldered in place.

EJECTOR, SHOP-BUILT RECEIVER

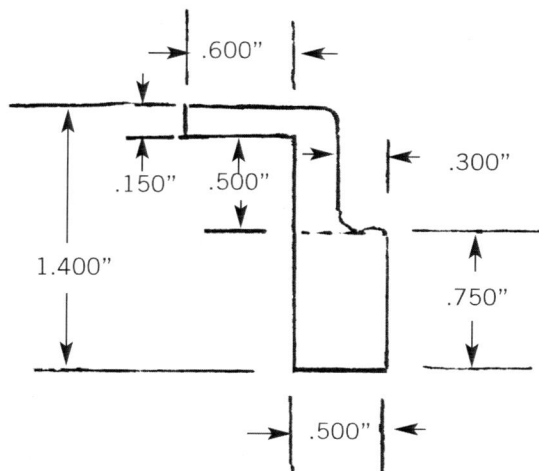

Diagram #35

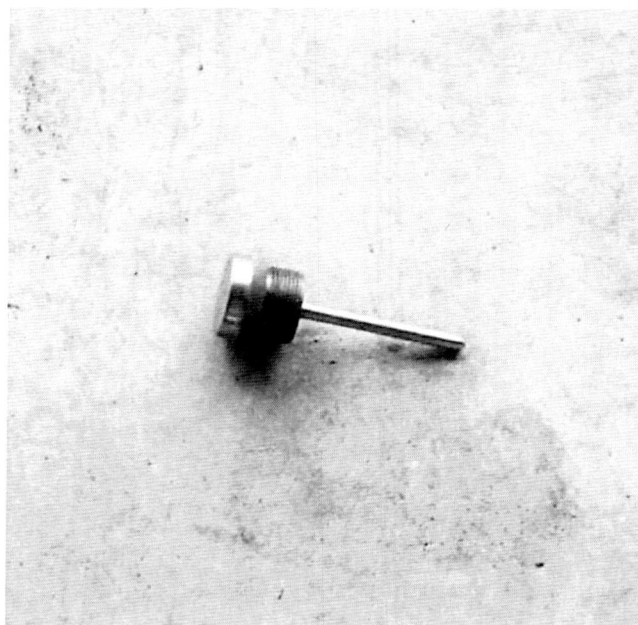

Breech plug used in open-bolt pistol version.

When the pistol version is built, a plug, or cap, should be made up to screw into the receiver opening, taking the place of the butt stock mount. If used as an open-bolt version, a single recoil spring guide is mounted in the center of the cap. This is done by drilling a 1/4-inch hole through the center of the cap and silver-soldering a suitable length of 1/4-inch drill rod in place. The inside of this cap is bored out, as shown in the drawing, to reduce weight. The knurled band on the largest diameter flange not only adds to the overall appearance but provides a gripping surface to aid in installing or removing the part.

When used as the closed-bolt version, the cap is made to the same overall configuration and dimensions except that the recoil spring guide is omitted. This version requires the same guide, made for two springs, as used in the short-bolt rifle version. This one is made by drilling two .156-inch diameter holes, which match the width of the spring holes in the bolt, through a thin plate of 3/16-inch flat stock. The ends of two matching lengths of 5/32-inch-diameter drill rod are inserted in these holes and silver-soldered in place.

In my prototype gun, I used two military M1 Carbine action springs in the closed-bolt version.

These are too long in their original state and must be cut off, a little at a time, until the bolt will open far enough to pick up cartridges from the magazine. I cannot tell you exactly how long these springs should be since varying dimensions, such as the depth of the holes in the bolt, and varying thickness of the wire used in the springs will have an effect.

For the open-bolt version, I used a spring obtained from an auto parts store. This one measures .375 inch in diameter, is wound from .050-diameter wire, and was originally 7/12 inches long. This one too was shortened, a little at a time, until the action would open completely. As with the closed-bolt version, this is strictly a "cut and try" proposition.

Extractors are identical for all three versions. Each should be cut from a better grade of material than common sheet metal, due to the fact that the hooked end must jump over the rim of each and every cartridge fed through the gun. Needless to say, if soft material is used the part will wear and deform rapidly. Leaf spring material can be milled to the required 1/8-inch thickness, or a thin slice can be cut from the end of an axle. Do not neglect this if you expect to use the gun extensively. As with most other small parts, this

.156" DIA. SPRING GUIDES

.200"

.800"

1.050"

2.700"

.650"

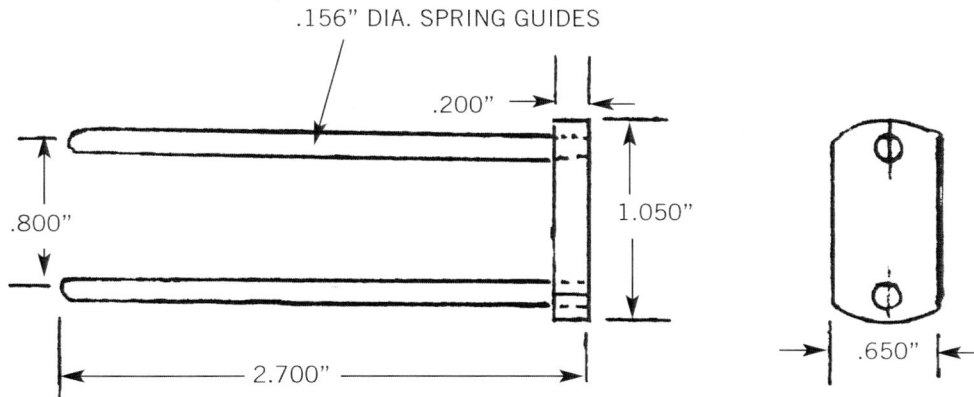

RECOIL-SPRING GUIDES, CLOSED-BOLT VERSION   Diagram #36

EXTRACTOR SAME FOR BOTH BOLTS

MADE FROM .125" THICKNESS, HEAT-TREATABLE STEEL. HOOK SHOULD BE MADE OVERSIZE AND FITTED TO SNAP OVER THE CARTRIDGE RIM DURING ASSEMBLY.

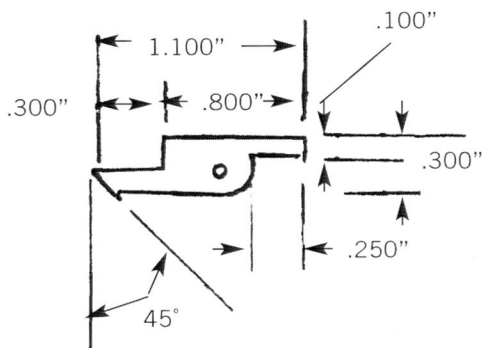

.100"

1.100"

.300"

.800"

.300"

.250"

45°

.087" PIVOT PIN HOLE SHOULD BE DRILLED THROUGH BOLT AND EXTRACTOR SIMULTANEOUSLY.

part should be made slightly oversize and dressed to exact fit during assembly.

If the closed-bolt configuration is adhered to, commercial firing mechanism components, which include a hammer, trigger, disconnector, safety, and necessary springs, are available from commercial and surplus parts sources. These are available at attractive enough prices to make it more sensible to buy them than to build them. Unfortunately, several of the surplus parts suppliers got the idea in their heads that they could rip off consumers by doubling, or sometimes tripling, the price of these small parts when the assault weapons ban went into effect. This, of course, didn't work out since there were many more such parts available than there was demand for them. As a result, prices have again returned to normal and should remain so for years to come. An example of this is that all required firing mechanism parts can be obtained from dependable parts suppliers such as Quality Parts Co. in Windham, Maine, for around $40. These are new parts, and Quality Parts ships promptly, without any B.S. or excuses.

Diagram #37

89

The open-bolt version will require manufacture of a sear, trigger, and disconnector. These are designed to interchange with the closed-bolt parts, using the existing pivot pins and pin holes, with no change in the lower receiver. This system uses a combination trigger bar and disconnector, which is hinged to the sear. The lower end of this part engages a projection protruding from the forward end of the trigger. Consequently, when the trigger is pulled to the rear the sear is pulled downward, out of engagement with the bolt, allowing the bolt to travel forward, pushing a cartridge from the magazine into the chamber. At the forward end of the bolt stroke, the firing pin crushes the primer, causing the round to fire. At this point, a combination of recoil and gas pressure causes the bolt to move to the rear, ejecting the fired case in the process, where it is again caught by the sear and held in the rearward, or cocked, position until another pull of the trigger causes the cycle to be repeated. The "lump," or projection, at the top of the trigger bar is depressed by the forward-moving bolt, which moves the lower, hooked end of the bar out of engagement with the trigger. This requires allowing the trigger to move forward again before a subsequent shot can be fired.

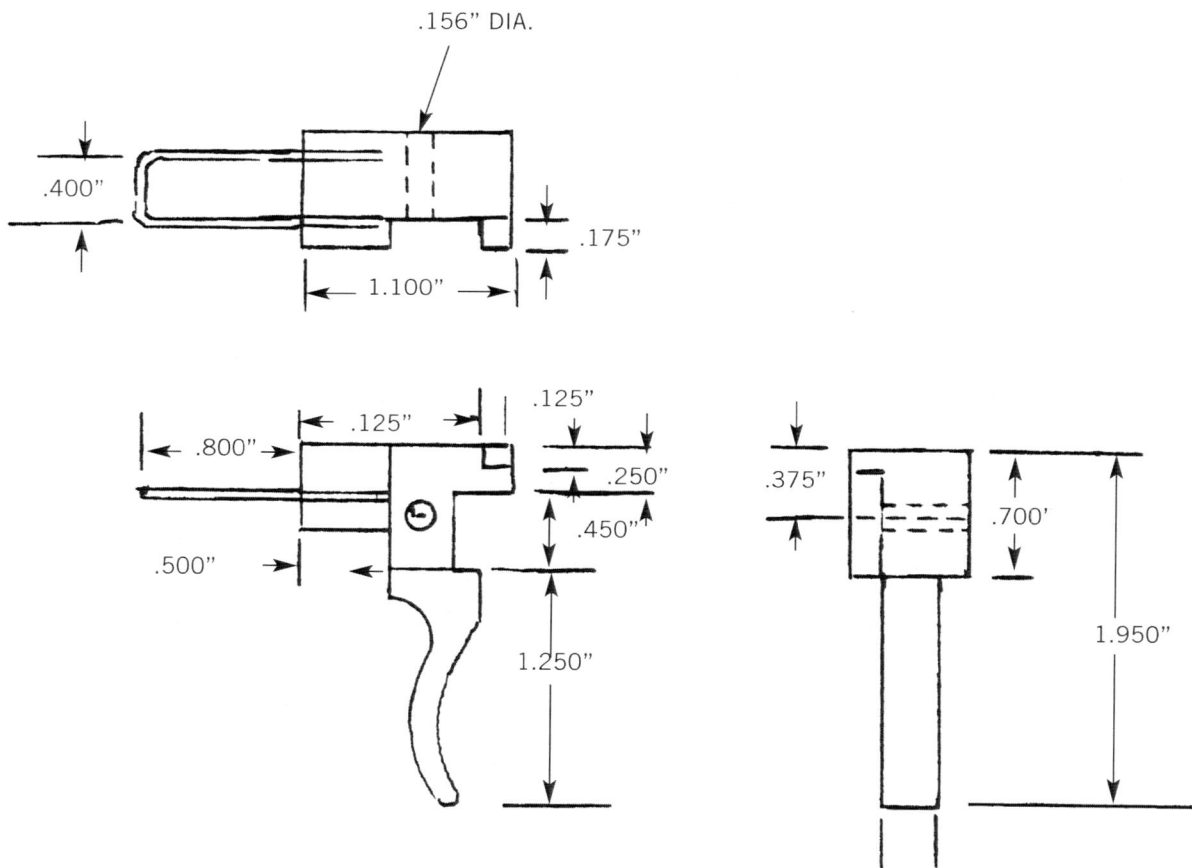

Diagram #38

TRIGGER (OPEN BOLT)

DETENT MADE FROM .187 DIA. DRILL ROD

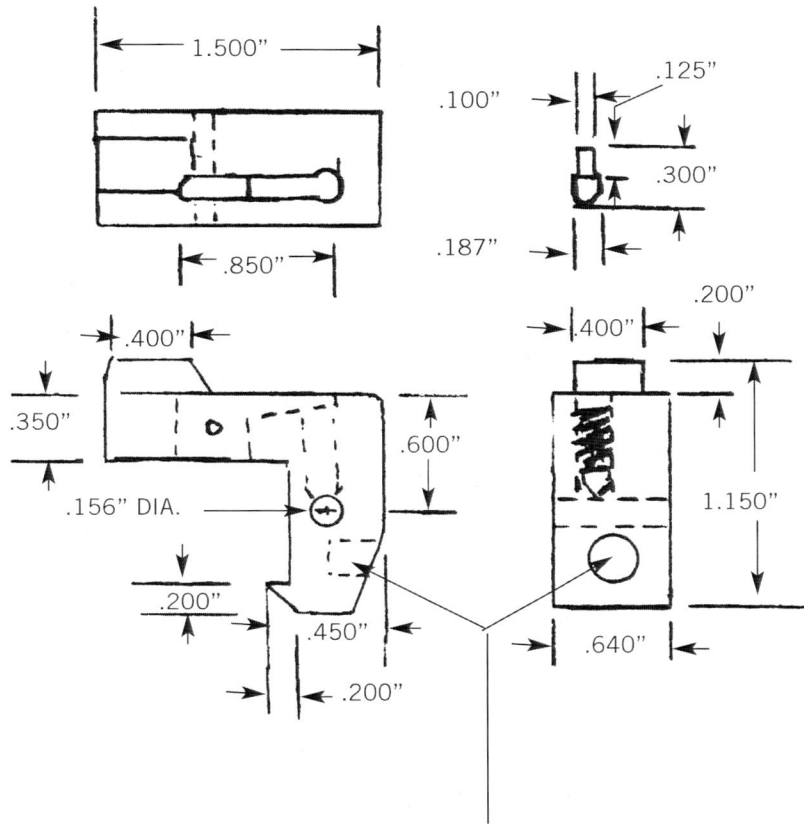

1.500"

.100"

.125"

.300"

.850"

.187"

.400"

.200"

.350"

.600"

.156" DIA.

1.150"

.200"

.450"

.640"

.200"

SPRING POCKET .250" DIA., .300" DEEP

SEAR (OPEN BOLT)

Diagram #39

91

THIS PART IS MADE FROM .125-INCH-THICKNESS,
HEAT-TREATABLE STEEL. IT SHOULD BE MADE
SLIGHTLY OVERSIZE AND FITTED DURING ASSEMBLY.

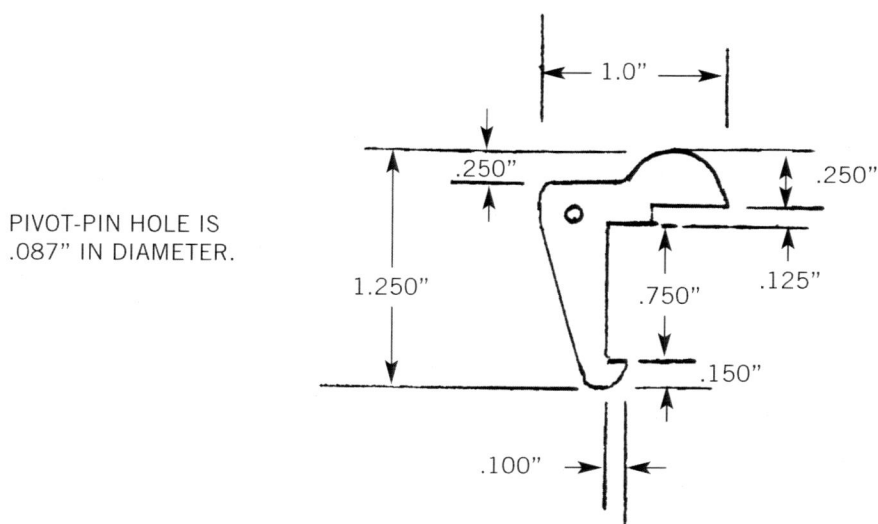

PIVOT-PIN HOLE IS
.087" IN DIAMETER.

1.0"
.250"
.250"
1.250"
.750"
.125"
.150"
.100"

Diagram #40   **TRIGGER DRAWBAR AND DISCONNECTOR**

Full automatic fire is achieved by pulling the trigger farther to the rear, against the pressure exerted by the U-shaped wire spring located at the rear of the trigger. This causes the forward end of the trigger to contact a projection located on the lower end of the sear, which, if the trigger is held back, holds the sear out of engagement with the bolt, allowing it to move forward and back unimpeded. This causes full automatic fire.

The sear is cut from 5/8 (.625)-inch-thick steel plate. This must be of a type that is shock-resistant and capable of heat treatment. As usual, 4140 or 4340 will serve admirably for this. Note that the disconnector spring bears against the

pivot pin, providing friction to hold it in place. The disconnector spring is 3/16 inch in diameter, wound from .018-inch wire, and the uncompressed length is between .300 and .400 inch. The sear spring, located in the lower front side, can be a section cut from the M1 Carbine recoil spring used in the closed-bolt version.

The trigger is made from the same material with a projection at the forward end on the right side to engage the trigger bar/disconnector. Two small 1/16-inch-diameter holes are drilled in the location shown to accept the U-shaped wire spring, which is formed from .065-inch music wire. This spring bears against the lower side of

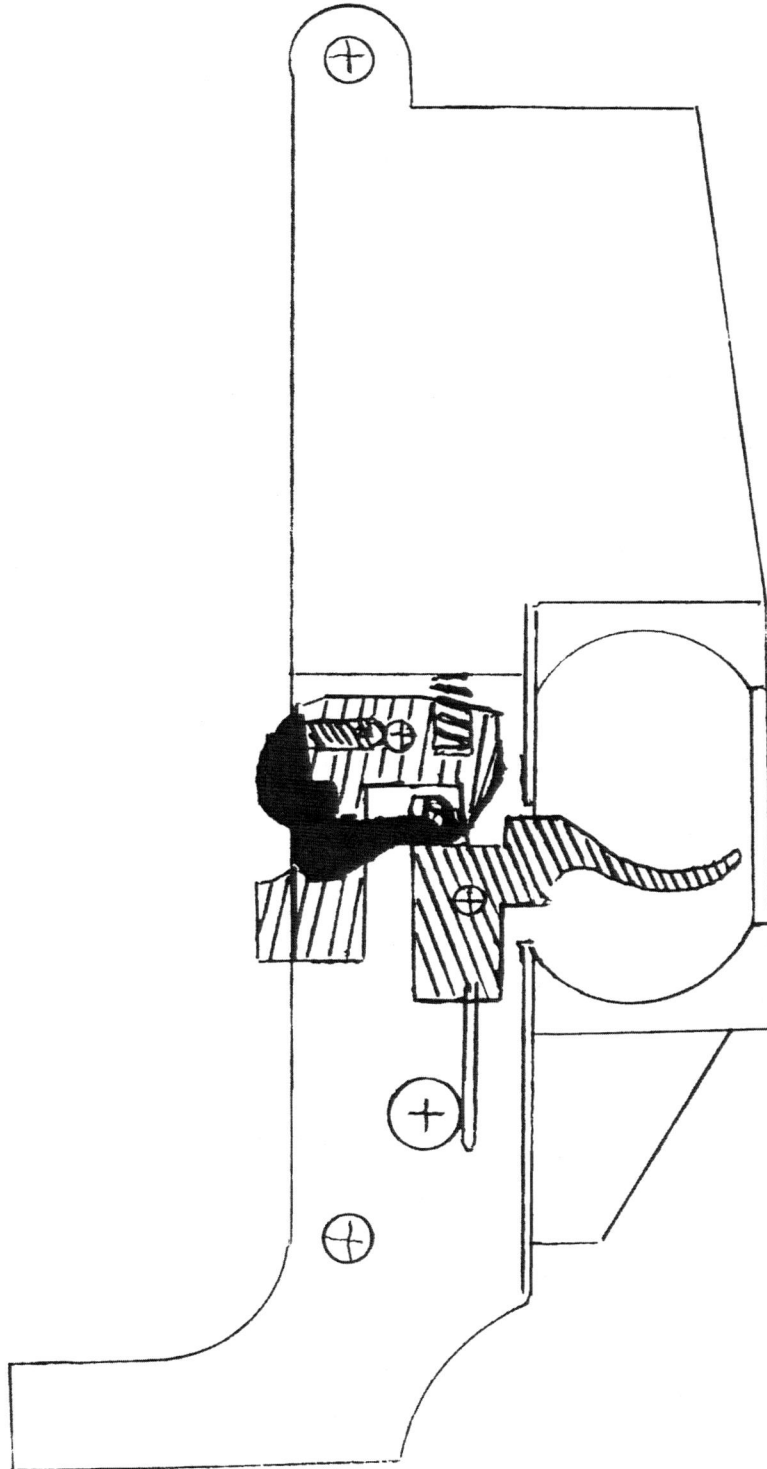

Diagram #41

the safety shaft, providing resistance to rearward movement of the trigger after the first, or semiautomatic, stage.

The trigger bar should be made from similar material, except that it is only 1/8 inch thick. Both the hook at the bottom and the lump at the top should be left slightly oversize to allow fitting during assembly.

For use in the closed-bolt version, an original firing pin can hardly be improved on. Here again, one can be purchased for less than the cost to make one. A drawing is included, however, in the event that manufacture should be required. Drill rod will suffice as material for this. Stems from automobile engine valves or shock absorber shafts can also be used. The experienced lathe operator will know to use a sharp cutting tool, set exactly on center, taking light cuts. Those who have never done this before may gain some valuable, although unpleasant, experience when making a part such as this.

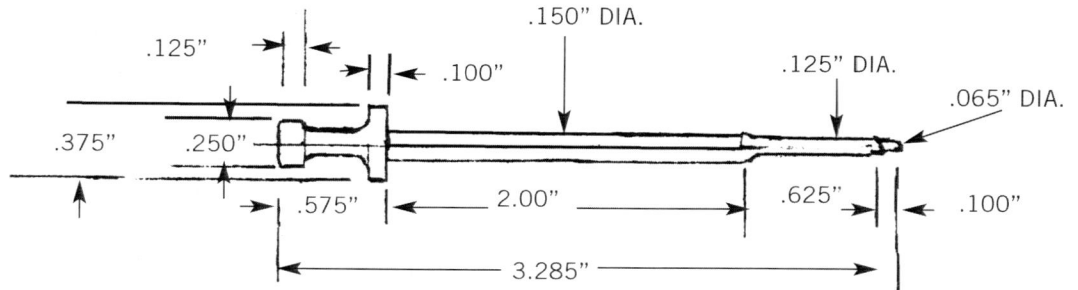

Diagram #42   **FIRING PIN**

FITTING AND ASSEMBLY

Before heat-treating and final finishing are performed, the parts should be assembled and any further fitting done as needed.

Assembly of the upper unit is begun by inserting the barrel tenon into the forward end of the upper receiver and screwing the barrel shroud, or fore-end, in place, which, when tightened against the flange of the barrel, holds it in place. The front sight is put in place and the retainer pin holes enlarged with a 3-0 taper pin reamer. Corresponding taper pins can be turned from 3/16-inch drill rod. Actually, it is a fairly simple matter to form the taper on these with a flat file while spinning each in the lathe. These pins are not installed permanently until after final finishing.

The firing pin and return spring are inserted in the bolt and the retaining pin installed. Firing pin protrusion should be .055 to .060 inch. This can be checked by holding the base of the firing pin flush with the bolt slot and measuring protrusion from the bolt face with a depth micrometer or vernier caliper. A 3/16-inch-diameter coil spring wound from .018-.022-inch-diameter wire is placed in the spring pocket, followed by the extractor, which is pinned in place. The spring must be short enough to allow the extractor hook to snap over the cartridge rim while retaining enough tension to hold it against the bolt face. It is a good idea to start with a

longer spring than necessary and cut it off, a coil at a time, until it works the way it is supposed to. The outer surface of the extractor body should be flush with, or slightly below, the surface of the bolt body. The front tip must not rub against the barrel slot.

The assembled bolt is now pushed in place through the rear of the receiver until the hole for the cocking lever lines up with the receiver opening, allowing the cocking lever to be put in place. The recoil springs are placed over their respective guides, and the assembly installed with the springs in their corresponding holes in the bolt. The unit is now ready for installation on the lower receiver.

The open-bolt pistol version is assembled in the same manner except that the fixed firing pin is already in place and requires no assembly, and the single recoil spring and guide are used.

Lower receiver parts are assembled in identical fashion in both the commercial and the manufactured versions, except that the magazine adaptor must be used in all commercial versions and those of the manufactured version having a full-size magazine opening. The smaller magazine opening version requires only that a small coil spring (a short length of the carbine recoil spring works well for this) be placed over the spring guide and the latch pinned in place. The trigger/disconnector and hammer are pinned in place and the safety installed. There should be no functional problems with the firing mechanism when used in the commercial version. Assuming that the pivot pin holes were drilled in the exact locations specified, the manufactured version should work equally well. If, however, you did not adhere closely to the locations shown, (remember, I warned you about this earlier), all sorts of problems may result.

If the hammer and trigger pins are too far apart, the disconnector quite likely won't work. This can usually be corrected by building up the forward ends of both the trigger and disconnector slightly by welding and reshaping them. If the holes are too close together, the hammer will not remain in the cocked position and/or the disconnector will not release the hammer. This can usually be corrected by shortening the trigger nose and/or the disconnector where it engages the hammer notch. This will only work if only a slight variation exists. Otherwise, the easiest out will be to weld up the holes and redrill them—in the right place this time.

The open-bolt trigger assembly is installed by first pinning the trigger in place, with the tail end of the U-shaped spring bearing against the underside of the safety. This spring causes extra resistance as the trigger is pulled farther to the rear, causing a definite step between the fairly light first stage, or semiautomatic, pull and the progressively harder second stage, whereby when the trigger is pulled farther to the rear, full automatic fire is accomplished. The original safety, as used in the closed-bolt version, is inoperative in this instance.

With a short length of 3/16-inch-diameter coil spring, wound from .016- to .020-inch wire, placed over the detent and installed in the spring pocket, the trigger bar/disconnector is put in place through the slot in the trigger and pinned. A short length of coil spring, cut from the excess portion of the carbine recoil spring, is placed in the spring pocket at the lower front of the sear and the sear is pinned in place. A small amount of wheel bearing grease deposited in spring pockets such as this will keep the springs from falling out while the part is being installed—not only in this instance, but many others as well.

With the parts in place, the hook at the lower end of the trigger bar must move forward under the projection at the front of the trigger. If this doesn't happen, material must be removed from either the hook or the trigger until it does. The lump at the top of the trigger bar will also require fitting at this point. As the bolt moves forward, the full-diameter portion rides over and depresses this lump, which, in turn, moves the hook at the lower end out of engagement with the trigger. This disconnects it, allowing the sear to engage and hold the bolt at the end of its rearward travel, even though the trigger is still held to the rear. The trigger must be released and allowed to move forward before a second shot can be fired.

When the trigger is pulled farther to the rear, the front edge engages a ledge at the bottom of the sear and holds it out of engagement with the bolt. This causes full automatic fire. It is desirable that the trigger have at least 1/8 inch of free travel between the point where it disconnects and the point where the sear ledge is depressed by the trigger nose. This is obtained by removing material from either the lower side of the trigger nose or the upper side of the sear ledge.

After the grip and butt stock are added (if assembled as a rifle), both receivers are joined by first pinning both together with the front hinge pin. The rear mounting bracket is inserted in the rear of the upper receiver and the rear pin installed. When used as the pistol version, the receiver cap, or plug, together with the corresponding recoil spring, is threaded in place in the rear of the receiver assembly instead of the butt stock.

The action should be cycled by hand several times, and if binding or excessive friction is present, the cause should be identified and eliminated. Proper functioning of the disconnector should be checked by hand-cycling the action with the trigger held back. The hammer must not fall or the open bolt move forward at the end of each cycle until the trigger is released and pulled again.

If you have built both versions, the closed-bolt assembly should be used to check for proper feeding. If only the open-bolt version is made up, a few dummy cartridges, consisting of a bullet seated in a sized case and without powder or primer, should be used. If live rounds are used to test feeding in this version, they will fire when the bolt slams closed.

With a single round in place in the magazine, the bolt is retracted and allowed to slam forward unimpeded, just as it would in actual firing. The cartridge should feed smoothly into the chamber, and when the bolt is again retracted, the cartridge should be withdrawn from the chamber and ejected as the bolt nears the end of its rearward travel. If the cartridge does not feed properly, try letting the bolt go forward slowly, observing where the bullet encounters interference. If it hits below the barrel approach cone, the magazine lips should be spread open slightly, allowing the cartridge to rise slightly higher in the magazine. If it strikes too high, the forward ends of the lips should be bent inward slightly. If the bullet nose hits on either side, move the lip on the same side inward slightly and the opposite side outward a like amount. It should be stated, however, that when a new magazine and the angled approach cone system detailed here are used, feeding problems are seldom encountered. If the single round feeds and ejects in the manner expected, the action should be cycled with three or more rounds in the magazine and adjustments made if required.

Close attention should be paid to head spacing, especially if the firearm is to be used extensively. Although a blowback action, as used here, can probably be fired safely with either insufficient or excessive head space, problems may occur further down the line. For instance, if the chamber is even as little as .010 inch short of being deep enough, the forward end, or mouth, of the case, which is what stops forward movement of the cartridge in the chamber, will slam against the end of the chamber with considerable violence. It is possible that the case may batter or deform at the mouth, which could pinch the bullet, raising chamber pressure to a dangerous degree. The chambered cartridge should have from .003 to .008 inch of clearance (head space) between the cartridge head and the bolt face.

Conversely, if the chamber is too deep, misfires may occur and case heads may separate from the bodies. It should also be noted that if the chamber is cut too deep, even as little as .020 inch, the gun will probably not fire at all, especially in the open-bolt version. The fixed firing pin simply does not indent the primer deep enough to crush it.

I am aware that in recent times certain pseudo-experts have expounded a theory of "advanced primer ignition," whereby, as they tell it, the cartridge in the process of being chambered is slowed by friction to a point where the firing pin ignites the primer before the action is completely closed. This is supposed to serve as a sort of hesitation lock, delaying the opening of the action. This is pure and simple conjecture on their part, since, in actual practice, the cartridge must come to a positive stop before the firing pin can impact the primer with sufficient force and depth to detonate it. This simply won't work in a firearm of this type.

I learned the truth of this several years ago when I was actively engaged in building and marketing an open-bolt 9mm assault pistol. One of my employees was assigned the task of chambering the barrels. This should have been a fairly simple, straightforward task since the chamber reamer was fitted with a stop collar, which should have limited the depth of the cut. Some way, however, my man managed to cut the chambers approximately .030 inch too deep. When these barrels were used on assembled guns and test-firing was attempted, not a single one of them would fire. I was required to remove a like amount of metal from the front of the bolt bodies of each of the affected guns, which let the bolts move forward far enough to take up the excessive head space. This proves, to me at least, that the theory of friction slowing the case to a point where "advanced primer ignition" occurs is just that—a theory, which doesn't work.

Once the gun is assembled and tentatively working the way it should, it should be disassembled and final polishing and heat-treating of parts requiring it should be performed before actual firing is attempted.

HEAT-TREATING AND FINISHING

The bolt, as well as the sear, trigger, and trigger bar for the open-bolt version, should be heat-treated. This is done primarily to prevent battering, or deformation, and rapid wear. Commercial parts obtained from reputable sources are already heat-treated and require no further attention.

Since I have discussed the principles of heat treatment in several other volumes, there is little point in repeating it here. All that is required is to thoroughly heat the steel parts to a temperature slightly above their critical stage, followed by cooling them quickly by plunging them into a quenching bath consisting of water, oil, brine, or other liquid as specified. Correctly done, this will result in a part (or parts) with a surface so hard a file won't touch it. It is also extremely brittle in this condition—so much so that even a small amount of shock may crack or break it. This condition is remedied by once more heating the parts to between 300 and 1290 degrees and allowing them to cool slowly. The exact temperature required for this "drawing," or "tempering," will vary considerably, depending on the composition of the steel, the carbon content, and the hardness desired.

The bolt(s) in this project should be heat-treated simply to prevent battering or deformation. Since this is a blowback action that is never actually locked, shear strength is not a determining factor. If commercial 4140 or 4340 is used for this, the heat treatment is fairly straightforward. The part should be heated to between 1450 and 1550 degrees, held there long enough to be certain that the part is completely saturated with a uniform temperature, and quenched in a bath of SAE #10 nondetergent motor oil (or similar) which is at or slightly above room temperature. This should result in a surface so hard that a file will simply skate across it without cutting. This, of course, would be ideal for wear resistance. However, any contact points subject to even a small amount of shock would soon crack or break. So, we must draw the temper at a temperature of approximately 800 degrees, which will soften it slightly but also put quite a bit of toughness back into it. This is done by again heating the part to the specified temperature and allowing it to cool slowly. If no specific temperature control is present, the part should be heated until it passes through a dark blue color and begins to turn green, at which point it is allowed to cool.

If using axle material or similar, you probably won't know the exact composition of the steel, so a bit of experimenting may be required. A scrap of this same material is used for testing, and since most medium- and high-carbon steels require heating to between 1450 and 1650 degrees for hardening, try heating the scrap to a bright,

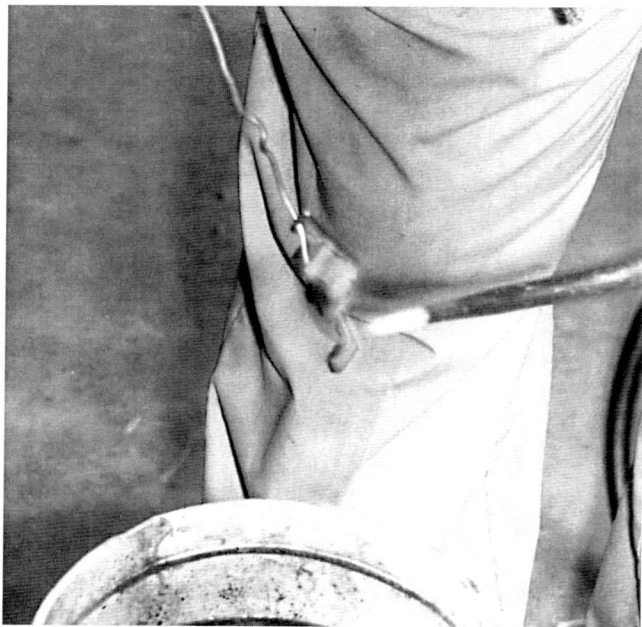

Small parts to receive heat-treatment are tied to heavy wire . . .

. . . heated to proper color . . .

. . . and quenched when desired color (usually bright cherry red) is reached.

Then temper is drawn by polishing bright, heating on steel plate.

glowing, cherry red and quenching it in the oil bath as described above. It should now be glass hard. If it is not, try the same, or another, scrap at a slightly higher temperature, and when the proper combination is found, apply it to the part to be hardened.

The small parts requiring same should be treated in similar fashion, except that they should be drawn at approximately 600 degrees. This is indicated by a dark blue color.

As I have stated in previous volumes, since I have no control over anyone's attempts at heat treatment other than my own, I cannot accept any responsibility for problems you may encounter.

With the heat-treatment done to your satisfaction, final polishing of all component parts should be done.

A dull, flat black finish is usually considered desirable for a paramilitary firearm of this type. When the upper assembly is used in connection with the commercial lower, such a finish will usually be similar to the anodized black finish used on the aluminum parts.

To obtain such a finish, the parts need not be polished to the degree required to obtain the bright blue finish used on sporting arms. Even so, all scratches, tool marks, and other blemishes should be removed. This can be done with power polishing equipment or by hand using files and abrasive cloth.

When the hand-polishing method is used, tool marks and blemishes are removed with a file. The round parts can be rotated in the lathe and tool marks removed by holding the file against the spinning part and moving it back and forth. This is followed by progressively finer grits of abrasive cloth, up to a final treatment with 320-grit wet or dry paper. This will be adequate for the finish used here. Flat parts are given the same file and followed by the same abrasive cloths wrapped around the file, wood blocks, dowels, or whatever it takes to contact and polish all exposed surfaces.

Following this, all exposed surfaces are subjected to a bead blast or sand blast treatment, which gives the metal a slightly roughened, frosted surface. Most machine shops and automotive paint and body shops have the

equipment to do this, and most will do it for a nominal charge.

Following this, the parts are degreased using one of the degreasing or detergent solutions found in grocery, paint, and hardware stores. A mild lye and water solution can also be used for this. After boiling for a few minutes in one of these solutions, followed by rinsing in clear water, they are ready for the bluing process. The parts should no longer be handled with the bare hands, since even the slightest smear of oil from your hands may have an adverse effect on the coloring process. Rubber gloves should be worn, or metal hooks or wires should be used to hold the parts.

In previous volumes I have described numerous methods and formulas used to impart the color desired. Any of these would be suitable for this project. Most of them have serious drawbacks for the one-time gun finisher in that they require either extensive equipment or a considerable amount of time to perform. In this book I will describe a couple of processes that may be useful when only a few parts are involved, since they require only a small outlay for materials and no equipment whatever.

One of these solutions is made by using as much copper sulfate—which is a bluish crystalline powder also known as bluestone or blue vitriol and available from drugstores—as 4 ounces of distilled water will dissolve. Fifteen to twenty drops of sulfuric acid should be added to this. The resulting solution is swabbed on the polished parts, which causes a copper plating action. A second coat will thicken the plating slightly. This is followed by a coat of sodium thiosulfide, which is used in processing film and can be found at photography stores. This will turn the copper black. Arsenic tri-oxide will work equally well for this. This process is also useful in that it will blacken stainless steel.

Another quick blue method is to first clean the metal with a solution of potassium bichromate-sulfuric acid mixture. The solution consists of 3 ounces of potassium bichromate (a chemical commonly used in photographic development and available at photo labs), 2 ounces of sulfuric acid, and 24 ounces of water. It is then washed with ammonium hydroxide and rubbed dry. A coat of ammonium polysulfide is next applied and allowed to dry while being rubbed briskly with a soft cloth. This is repeated until the desired color is reached. The resulting color is a deep blue, which will turn almost black with repeated applications. The color can be deepened still more by rubbing with boiled linseed oil. This results in a finish that is extremely rust-resistant but will not wear as well as the nitrate or rust blue finishes described earlier. Both of the finishes described here are, however, quick and cheap.

Both of these methods use sulfuric acid in at least one mixture. Therefore, rubber gloves and eye protection should be worn when applying.

The ammonium polysulfide mixture is a pale yellow liquid consisting of ammonium sulfide saturated with sulfur. The ingredients are available from chemical supply houses and older drug stores. I first used this process more than 50 years ago after discovering a description of the process in an old chemistry book. This was during World War II, when many chemicals used in bluing solutions were unavailable or in short supply. I prevailed upon a lovely young lady by the name of Bernice Hoffman, who was in one of our high school chemistry classes, to make me up some of this, and a couple of days later she handed over a bottle of each solution. This worked well enough that I used it exclusively until my supply ran out. By that time commercial solutions were once more available, so I went to them instead. I didn't make up any more until a short time ago when I got up another batch just to make sure it worked the way I remembered. It does, and if it were not for the rotten egg smell present when the bottle is open, I would go back to using it again for certain jobs.

Most of the metal coloring recipes, or formulas, that I have included in my books are old—at least 50 years or more. Some of them were old 50 years ago. Some of the chemicals are called by different names now, and some young druggists won't even know what you are talking about if you ask for them. Older druggists and chemists know about them, however, and most, or all, of them are still available—even though it may require a little effort to locate them.

FIRING AND ADJUSTING

With the component parts finished and colored to your satisfaction and reassembled, the project should be ready for test-firing. It might be assumed that, since the gun was assembled and semi test-fired before heat-treating and finishing and seemed to work the way it was supposed to, it will still do so. This may or may not be the case. Parts sometimes grow or otherwise change shape while being heat-treated. This can also happen when certain types of coloring techniques are practiced. Still others tend to etch the surface of the metal, leaving it slightly rough. In many cases, parts that moved freely around pivot pins during the first assembly will no longer do so.

When testing the closed-bolt version, make sure that the extractor will still open far enough to snap over the cartridge rim and hold the case head against the bolt face. If it does not, check for burrs or other roughness and make sure the pivot pin still works freely through the hold in the extractor.

The firing pin should be examined carefully to make sure that it doesn't stick in its forward position and that it retracts fully when not in contact with the hammer.

Don't overlook this. One time, earlier on, I carelessly assembled a bolt similar to the one used here, assuming that, since it worked before I blued it, it still would. When I inserted a magazine with two rounds in it, retracted the bolt, and let it slam forward, both rounds fired, even though the safety was engaged and the trigger wasn't touched. Subsequent examination revealed that a solidified lump of the nitrate salts I used to blue the gun was lodged in the firing pin hole and had jammed the firing pin in its forward position, effectively causing it to become a fixed firing pin. Another time I test-fired a 9mm pistol of similar design. This one had been fired numerous times several months before. It had worked perfectly then. But this time, when I let the bolt go forward, all five rounds in the magazine fired. Examination showed that the firing pin retracted just the way it was supposed to and moved back and forth without binding. When the action was cycled slowly by hand, the hammer remained cocked until the trigger was pulled. It was eventually discovered that the sear pivot pin had rusted, causing just enough drag that although the hammer remained cocked during the forward movement of the bolt, the jarring effect when the bolt slammed fully closed caused the hammer to slip off of the partially engaged sear. This, in effect, resulted in a closed-bolt, hammer-fired machine gun. These experiences prove three things: first, that I am not perfect; second, that I should have loaded only one round for test-firing, as I have advocated here; and third, that nothing should be taken for granted. Always check these things carefully, and when test-firing, keep the muzzle pointed downrange.

The first test-firing should be done by inserting

a magazine containing a single round, retracting the bolt, and allowing it to slam forward unimpeded, as it would in the firing cycle. It should push the round out of the magazine and into the chamber. Before firing is attempted, retract the bolt slightly to ascertain whether the extractor snapped in place over the cartridge rim. If it didn't, the spring is too stiff or there is mechanical interference, which should be corrected before test-firing proceeds further. This will usually be done by substituting a weaker extractor spring or locating and removing metal from the place where interference or contact occurs. Usually, coating the exposed extractor surfaces with lipstick or the like and working the bolt a couple of times with a cartridge in the chamber will show where the problem is.

If the bolt closes completely and the extractor works the way it is supposed to, the gun should be held so that it points away from you and any close spectators and the round fired. Ideally, the round will fire and the bolt will travel to the rear, ejecting the empty case in the process, and move again to the closed position.

Failure to fire can be caused by several things. Perhaps the firing pin is too short. This can be checked by removing the barrel, and, with the hammer forward against the base of the firing pin, measuring from the face of the receiver to the bolt face. Another measurement is taken from the face of the receiver to the protruding firing pin tip. This last measurement is subtracted from the first, and the result will be the amount of firing pin protrusion, which must be at least .055 inch. If it is not, the shoulder in the firing pin hole, which limits its forward travel, must be deepened a corresponding amount.

Failure to fire can be the result of the chamber being cut too deep, also known as excessive head space. (Go back and read what I said about this earlier.) This condition can be corrected by cutting back the front edge of the receiver an appropriate amount. This will allow the barrel to move farther back into the receiver. The same result can be achieved by cutting back the front face of the bolt body—not the small, counterbored bolt-nose portion, but the larger outer body. Either of these

actions will close the gap between the barrel and chamber and the bolt face, which, when done in the required amount, will correct the excessive head space.

As it turns out, though, the round does fire, due mainly to your precision workmanship and attention to detail. So we can now load two rounds and try it again. If both fire and eject, five rounds should be loaded and fired, followed by several loadings of not more than ten. Full magazine loadings should be postponed until a hundred rounds or more have been fired, which will tend to loosen up the action and smooth out any rough spots or burrs still present. A fully loaded magazine increases friction against the reciprocating bolt and may very well slow it to a point where it doesn't open completely. Thus, the break-in period to loosen it up.

It may very well be that even after a break-in period the action doesn't open completely when the magazine is fully, or almost fully, loaded. This is evidenced by failure to eject empty cases and/or failure of the bolt to open far enough to pick up the next round from the magazine. This can usually be cured by shortening the recoil springs, which should be done slowly, a coil or two at a time, test-firing each time, until the bolt opens completely. This too has its drawbacks, in that enough spring pressure must remain to close the bolt completely. So don't overdo it.

The open-bolt version is tested and adjusted in essentially the same way, except, of course, that inadequate firing-pin protrusion can be ruled out as a cause of failure to fire. This time, the bolt should remain open when it reaches the end of its rearward travel while in the semiautomatic mode. Its failure to do so can be caused by an overly stiff recoil spring. This is corrected the same way as was done with the closed bolt. Another cause of this can be that the sear face is angled forward, causing the bolt to cam it down and out of engagement. This surface, as well as the surface of the bolt it engages, must be square and flat.

As described earlier, full automatic fire is caused by simply pulling the trigger farther to the rear, which cams the sear out of engagement, rendering the disconnector inoperative.

CONCLUSION

I have mentioned several times before that any and all versions of this project would probably be considered illegal if built after the assault weapons law went into effect in 1994. My prototype gun is legal, since it was built before that date. At least the closed-bolt version is. I no longer have an open-bolt version or a pistol version. That the open-bolt version was successful can be demonstrated by the fact that BATF agents seized the one I had completed to illustrate this book and charged me in federal court with illegal machine gun manufacture. Fortunately, I was aware of what they had in mind from the beginning and I was acquitted. But they proved that the gun worked.

Since the muzzle of that particular version isn't threaded, if the bayonet lug were removed and the magazine cut off to where it would only hold 10 rounds, it may very well be that it would be legal. I wouldn't count on it, though. If federal agents catch you with any version of this gun and they think they can convince a jury that it was built after the cut-off date, they will very likely file a charge against you—or, at least, confiscate your weapon.

I think (note that I say, I *think*) that if only the upper assembly is built and attached to an existing lower, this would result in a legal weapon. But don't depend on it. This too could change at any time.

If the time should come, however, when you simply must have a weapon such as this for survival or defense, then it isn't going to make much difference what is legal and what isn't. Until that time comes, however, I suggest that you simply practice making parts. And maybe store some away to use in the future—although even that may be considered illegal by some. Do so at your own risk.